T0289948

PLATFORM STRATEGY

A New Paradigm for a Changing World

PLATFORM STRATEGY

A New Paradigm for a Changing World

Ki-Chan Kim

The Catholic University of Korea, South Korea

Chang Seok Song

Soongsil University, South Korea

Il Im

Yonsei University, South Korea

World Scientific

NEW JERSEY · LONDON · SINGAPORE · BEIJING · SHANGHAI · HONG KONG · TAIPEI · CHENNAI · TOKYO

Published by

World Scientific Publishing Co. Pte. Ltd.

5 Toh Tuck Link, Singapore 596224

USA office: 27 Warren Street, Suite 401-402, Hackensack, NJ 07601

UK office: 57 Shelton Street, Covent Garden, London WC2H 9HE

Library of Congress Cataloging-in-Publication Data

Names: Kim, Ki-Chan. | Song, Chang Seok. | Im, Il.

Title: Platform strategy : a new paradigm for a changing world / Ki-Chan Kim,
    Chang Seok Song, Il Im.

Description: New Jersey : World Scientific, [2019] | Includes index.

Identifiers: LCCN 2018056462 | ISBN 9789813277458 (hardback)

Subjects: LCSH: Technological innovations--Management. | Leadership.

Classification: LCC HD45 .K56 2019 | DDC 658.4/012--dc23

LC record available at https://lccn.loc.gov/2018056462

British Library Cataloguing-in-Publication Data

A catalogue record for this book is available from the British Library.

For any available supplementary material, please visit
https://www.worldscientific.com/worldscibooks/10.1142/11189#t=suppl

Desk Editor: Daniele Lee

Typeset by Stallion Press
Email: enquiries@stallionpress.com

Printed in Singapore

Foreword I

Platform Strategy: Not a Choice, but a Necessity

As the world undergoes a perpetual state of change, so must the principles of the business world. Adaptation to new environments in order to survive is necessary, not only for living organisms, but for business organizations and companies, too.

It is natural that business models should change over time. The stand-alone model in which everything was done by oneself was applicable during the eras of agrarian and early industrial societies, when the value chain systems were simpler. However, with evermore sophisticated information technologies, increasing competitiveness, and the constant need for creative innovation in many companies, it is no surprise that the stand-alone model is rapidly disappearing.

In early industrial society, the production of a good was based on one patent. However, in today's market, systems are often creatively combined, such that multiple patents are required for the creation of a single product. For example, in order to produce one smartphone, thousands of patent issues must be resolved. The competition in the smartphone market is the competition of creativity and innovation. In reality, it has become impossible for one company to control all of the patents associated with one product, and value chains that lack creativity, inevitably fall behind due to the natural selection process of the business world.

There is a solution to this problem: in this era of networks, companies must provide platforms that are full of change, creativity, innovation, and collaboration. They must provide solutions to business partners and become essential intermediaries in the market. Their platforms must become part of business ecosystems based on the ability to innovate. As active and leading members of new business ecosystems, they must let go of the old idea of solely protecting their own markets.

The company that controls the platform wins. No company can escape this new rule. This book provides clear explanations of platform strategy, focusing on two key words: "solution" and "serendipity". The various examples of platform strategy that are introduced in this book will help readers understand the nature of platforms and enable them to look at the business world with a fresh perspective.

Kwon, Oh-Hyun

Chairman, Samsung Electronics

Foreword II

The New World: Integration of Platforms and Business Ecosystems

Seventy percent of the world's economy depends on employment provided by small businesses. Therefore, the main focus of national economic policies should be to support these small businesses as drivers of future economic development.

Small businesses lack the resources to compete with large companies. To cultivate small businesses and help them realize their potential for future economic development, a base to provide social support and to help small businesses overcome this weakness is essential. Such a platform to support small businesses can be provided at a national level. For example, the Korean Trade-Investment Promotion Agency (KOTRA) is a platform by which the Korean government supports exports by small Korean businesses. Large companies can also provide a platform for small businesses by creating innovative ecosystems that allow them to coexist with small businesses, treating them as partners. As small businesses in the ecosystem gain expertise in niche technologies, open innovation among the companies in the network becomes possible, eventually leading to benefits for the large company that is providing the platform.

Integration between platforms and business ecosystems is becoming increasingly common. For instance, Uniqlo, which created a platform, is cultivating an ecosystem of originality, while Zara is expanding through its platform of innovation and constant production updates.

The platform has been evolving from merely an option for a healthy ecosystem into an essential business strategy to survive in today's business environment. Some explanation of the platform phenomenon has been provided with successful examples introduced, but a comprehensive understanding of various aspects of platforms from a business point of view is necessary. This book provides the definition of "platform" and describes the operation of platforms from both economic and business perspectives, listing some guidelines for successful platform strategy. Many examples of platforms in various fields throughout history are outlined. Most aspects of platform business are touched upon, and predictions are made about what platforms will look like in the future.

I happily recommend this book to readers who are both familiar and unfamiliar with the concept to improve their understanding of the platform phenomenon.

Kwak, Sukeun

Professor Emeritus,
Seoul National University,
Business School

Foreword III

Platforms Create Mega Synergy

Modern society is a hyper-connected society. The integration and convergence of many specialized fields has been evident throughout history. The impact of these convergences on the world is enormous. Converged creativity is especially noteworthy. If Edison is the model for the original notion of creativity, Steve Jobs is the one for converged creativity. Convergence is the hallmark of the "mega synergy" era. The simple formula of the past: $1 + 1 = 2 + \alpha$, is passing away. In fact, the $+\alpha$ concept, which has been emphasized in economics and management literature for decades, has limitations. However, the mega synergy created by the convergence of different products from different sectors in the modern era overcomes this limitation.

The success of newcomer companies such as Apple, Google, and Alibaba is due to the fact that they created this mega synergy. However, the phenomenon of convergence also has its downside. Conflict and contradiction among individual companies in independent fields has become common as they open up to one another. This is why it is said that we live in an "era of chaos and contradiction" which is difficult to resolve within the existing limits of logic and science.

What we need now is the convergence of knowledge and intelligence. The ability to look at the ecosystem as a whole and to understand the interplay among its various factors is essential. As I study this phenomenon more and more, I realize that collaboration is impossible if we do not understand the ecosystem as a whole. A holistic view of ecosystems and the world is crucial. Therefore, we need a new leader with a holistic view in this era of converged creativity.

I am so happy to see this timely book. I applaud the authors and their explanations of the concepts of ecosystems, converged creation, and talent within the clear framework of the platform. I recommend this book with the belief that it will be an important milestone for creative and economic development in Korea and in other countries.

Yoon, Eun-Ki

President, Korea Collaboration Association

Preface

Looking at the World Through the Lens of Platform

Throughout history, countries and organizations with high levels of openness, diversity, and tolerance have been rewarded with longevity. Openness characterized the Roman Empire, which lasted over a thousand years. Citizenship was offered to all people who were willing to spill their sweat and blood for Rome, regardless of where they had originated from. The Romans did not possess the intelligence of the Greeks, the physical strength of the Germans, the technological advancements of the Etruscans, and the financial astuteness of the Carthaginians. Therefore, the Roman government simply chose to provide a platform for these talents. The outcome of this platform strategy combined with Rome's openness was the development of Roman society in terms of education, economy, and military power.

On the other hand, the Qianlong Emperor of the Qing dynasty, who controlled more than half of the world's economy in the eighteenth century, led his country downhill with his closed-minded view on national boundaries. Historical records tell of his boasting about his winning streak over the course of ten wars. However, in reality, it was not something to boast about. He may have expanded his territory to the farthest extent possible, but the country's economy was ruined due to the frequency of these expensive wars. This is a clear example of how a closed platform and ecosystem can limit the evolution of an organization.

The platform is the starting point, the place in which people gather, the playground for members of the ecosystem. As a platform emerges, various elements of the ecosystem mature and flourish there. Thus, the wealth and the development of a country are directly proportional to the number of platforms that are under its control.

When Seoul Station first opened in 1925, travel to Seoul became much easier, which eventually contributed to the evolution of the financial, educational, and cultural ecosystems of Korea. The constructions of the Suwon, Cheonan, and Daejeon stations, which are respectively located 30 minutes away from the preceding station, resulted in the creation of a big metropolis; an engine of national development. In other words, the establishment of a platform in the form of transportation infrastructure led to the evolution of an ecosystem on the national level.

Let us re-visit Ancient Rome for a moment, where various platforms were created, thus leading to the success of many ecosystems. Whenever the Roman Empire had money, the Romans built roads rather than castles. The fascinating result of this principle was the development of 80,000 kilometers of roads throughout the Roman Empire. Citizens of the Roman Empire, including Greeks and Germans, utilized these roads with regularity, and soon gathering places appeared alongside these roads. These gathering places developed into platforms for economic activity (markets), education (schools), and health & exercise (baths). Ancient Rome prospered tremendously, based on these platforms. On the other hand, countries that dedicated most of their finances and their time to building gates instead of roads, were short-lived.

Obviously, platform development is one of the best formulas for the evolution of an organization. Platforms have often been associated with certain physical spaces that are too big to be controlled by anyone other than the government. Therefore, historically governments have established and managed platforms, extracting fees and rent from the people. However, in the era of the Internet and mobile devices, expensive physical platforms are no longer necessary. Virtual platforms have replaced physical platforms. Platform management is commensurate with this change and has transferred to the private domain.

Platform strategy has proven useful in various fields. A huge number of businesses provide virtual platforms through the Internet and mobile systems, making profit from fees for platform use. Thus, it is appropriate to view the world from the perspective of platform development.

Our initial focus is on solutions and serendipity, because these are key elements of platform strategy. We call these PASS1 (platform as a set of solutions) and PASS2 (platform as a serendipitous strategy) for easy distinction. To develop a platform, a solution must be offered related to the problems of people who visit the platform. When people visit, they must find serendipity in the solutions provided by the platform. People who come to the platform for solutions will visit again if they find serendipity. With more people visiting the platform and thus generating involvement, the more the ecosystem will prosper, and the more business will develop.

Prologue

A Fun and Exciting Platform

What image comes to mind when you hear the word "platform"? You probably think of a train station. The dictionary defines a platform as "a raised structure from which passengers can enter or leave a train". In addition to this dictionary definition, we may have emotional associations of the word, platform, in relation to travel, meeting, and farewell.

The term "platform" in this book is, of course, related to neither the dictionary definition, nor any of the possible emotional connotations of the word. We discuss platform strategy, which is a new and popular topic in management research. However, since we are talking about platforms, let us think about the first true motion picture, *Arrival of a Train at La Ciotat*.[1] This is a short film which lasts less than one minute. La Lumière held the first public screening of a film at which admission was charged at the Salon Indien du Grand Café. This history-making presentation featured 10 short films. This film, *Arrival of a Train at La Ciotat*, left a particularly strong impression on viewers. Why?

There was no extraordinary action in the movie other than people entering and leaving the train after its arrival. However, people screamed and even ran away during the arrival scene, because they

---

[1] Original title: *L'arrivèe d'un train à la Ciotat*, arguably the first film in the world. It would be more appropriate to call it the first commercial film, since admission fees were charged to view it.

had never been exposed to film. This film subsequently became famous through word of mouth.

People were excited by the *Arrival of a Train at La Ciotat*, because they found serendipity. We will explain further how important serendipity is for platform strategy.

The miracle of the 2002 World Cup can be understood in terms of serendipity. It was unexpected for Korea to be ranked 4th in the World Cup. The main factor that contributed to this outcome was that the Korean Soccer Association (KSA) hired Guus Hiddink as coach. Hiddink reformed the Korean soccer team and reformulated the ecosystem of Korean soccer. He scouted new talents and led sleepy people to the plaza in front of City Hall to see the broadcast. The plaza became a platform of excitement that induced serendipity. It was not intentional, but the PASS2 (platform as a serendipitous strategy) was successful.

If the KSA had stuck to a stand-alone strategy and selected established players only, or adopted a policy of interference, Korea might have failed even at the preliminary stage of the games. However, the KSA stepped back after hiring Hiddink and allowed him to handle the team as he wished. As a result, the Korean soccer ecosystem evolved drastically.

Hiddink adopted the role of an evangelist. Of course, we do not refer to the dictionary definition of this word. Some employees at companies like Apple and Google have the word "evangelist" written on their business cards as part of their job description. In business contexts, evangelists are diplomats who handle external relations and recruit players from various industries and markets to their own company platforms. These evangelists form partnerships with product developers, and products such as applications improve the competitiveness of the platform. iTunes for the iPod and the App Store for the iPhone are excellent examples. Apple provides the platform, and its evangelists cultivate the business ecosystem to make the company grow.

There is however, an opposite example. Napster, which developed innovative technology to help music lovers enjoy their music, totally ignored the interests of music producers. Napster's management chose a stand-alone strategy instead of a platform strategy. The result was their disappearance from the MP3 music market.

Apple, on the other hand, adopted a platform strategy, thereby creating a win-win ecosystem for everybody with the same technology. The outcome was the sale of over three hundred million iPods. Apple's success may be attributed to its creation of a business ecosystem in partnership with music producers through iTunes, based on the philosophy, "don't steal the music." As a result, Apple products made by partners within the ecosystem improved competitiveness based on the platform strategy.

At this juncture, it is important that we highlight one particular point; the term "business ecosystem" has been mentioned several times already. The concept of business ecosystem is equally significant to the concepts of serendipity and platform strategy throughout this book.

To be brief, this book is written from the standpoint that the business ecosystem is the framework of the business world. Within the business world, competition occurs not only between individual companies, but also between the ecosystems in which those companies belong.

The core measure of success in the business ecosystem is the platform. A company can survive competition and create value when it has a better platform or makes better use of a platform than its rivals. For example, in the smartphone market, the competition seems to be between two major companies: Samsung and Apple. However, the real competition is between the Android system and the iOS system. Google and Samsung are both part of the business ecosystem surrounding the Android platform, and the iOS platform is the base of Apple and Foxconn. Therefore, Apple and Google are competing not in terms of hardware sales, but in terms of the success of their platforms and the expansion of their business ecosystems. In this book, competition between these business ecosystems is referred to as platform competition. Companies that are successful in their platform strategies are those that create exciting heroes; the excitement they generate leads to the evolution of the ecosystem.

What about your company? Is it constantly producing heroes? Do you have evangelist generals who are engaged in battle in the fierce, global ecosystem war? Are you recruiting ten righteous evangelists who will jump into the fire pit? Or are you an over-controlling president with misplaced pride in your own technology, as depicted in the cautionary tale of Napster?

PLATFORM

Professor Marco Iansiti of Harvard University defines the platform as a "group of solutions in which members of the ecosystem approach through many meeting points and the interface". While this is an attractive definition, it may be easier for us to understand the platform concept by examining some familiar cases. Let us therefore explore platforms in various fields with consideration of two key words: "interface" and "solution".

Railway Platform

This is the place we get on and off the train. The railway platform is the place passengers must go through to get where they want to go (solution). The platform must be near and accessible (interface). For example, comparing Gimpo Airport and Incheon Airport, Incheon offers more air routes (solution), but Gimpo is more accessible (interface). Which is the better airport for a trip to Shanghai?

Base Camp

The number of successful climbers of Mount Everest, which has an elevation of 8,848 meters, is exponentially increasing. Why? It is true that the development of mountain climbing techniques and better information has contributed to this increase. However, the most significant contributor is the shift of base camp up to the height of 6,200 meters. After the establishment of this base camp, mountaineers could start their climbing expeditions from the height of 6,200 meters. This is the reason behind the increasing interest in climbing Mount Everest.

(Continued)

(Continued)

On the Shoulders of Giants

Isaac Newton quoted an old adage, saying, "If I have seen farther, it is by standing on the shoulders of giants". In other words, however fantastic any scholastic accomplishment may be, it would be impossible without the accumulation of knowledge throughout history. In that sense, "on the shoulders of giants" can be interpreted as referring to a platform.

Computing Platform

When an application runs on a certain computer operating system such as Windows or LINUX, we call that operating system its platform. The operating system has all the functions required for the applications to work, and the applications then add their own unique functions. To work smoothly, the interplay between the operating system and the applications should be simple (interface).

Automobile Platform

An automobile platform consists of a set of closely connected parts and essential automobile components, typically those located in the lower body and suspension, shared by many car models. For example, the Renault auto company utilizes the same design, engine, and transmission for its cars in every country, making small changes in detail depending on the particular needs in each country. This approach is frequently applied to other products. Platform standardization accomplishes economies of scale, at the same time making it easier to adapt the product to local circumstances.

Connection Platform

Credit card companies connect card users with the stores in which they make purchases. A computer operating system connects the user with the developer. A matchmaker connects a man with a woman. An online keyword advertising system connects the advertiser with the consumer. A job search website connects the employer and the job seeker. Intermediaries that connect two or more markets are called connection platforms.

Contents

Forewords
  I   Platform Strategy: Not a Choice, but a Necessity   v
  II The New World: Integration of Platforms and
       Business Ecosystems   vii
  III Platforms Create Mega Synergy   ix

Preface
Looking at the World Through the Lens of Platform   xi

Prologue
A Fun and Exciting Platform   xv

Part I Why Platform Now?   **1**
Chapter 01   A New Business Model   3

  Using Platforms for Play   5
  Various Definitions of Platform   6
  Traditional Platforms   9
    Credit Card   10
    Newspapers   10
    Video Games   11
    Matchmaking Business   12
  Is a Department Store a Platform?   13
    The Department Store as a Solution   13
    The Department Store as a Two-Sided Market   14

Economic Perspectives on Platforms   15
Platform: A New Business Model   17
Insist on Piping or Transform into Platform?   18

Chapter 02   Platform Operation and the Open Ecosystem   21

Operation of the Platform   23
    Platform Composition   23
    The Roles of Platform Participants   24
Platform Ecosystems   26
    The Crisis of Business Education   26
    No More Competition   27
    Welcome Everybody   28
    The Software in the End   29

Chapter 03   Two Pillars of Value Creation by the Platform   33

Everybody Shares   35
Hand in Hand   36
Cross-Network Value   38

Chapter 04   Successful Companies with Platform Businesses   41

Companies with Platforms on the Internet   43
    Pioneer of the Mobile Platform: The Apple App Store   43
    Destroying Borders: Facebook Connect   43
    Open Platforms in Electronic Commerce   44
Companies with Offline Platforms   45
    An Ecosystem of Wide Scope: Walmart   45
        The Secret of Walmart's Success   46
        The Development of the Walmart Platform:
            Retail Link®   46
        The Effect of Walmart's Platform   48
        Walmart's Second-Generation Platform   48
    The Store is the Platform   49
        The Birth of the Specialty Department Store: JCPenney   49
        Come and Touch It: Best Buy   51
    The Evolution of Collaboration: Open Innovation   52

Must We Develop for Ourselves?: P&G   52
Trade the Technology: InnoCentive   54
Why Open Innovation?   55
Platform Strategy for the Latecomer: Xiaomi   56
Software as a Competitive Weapon   57
Profiting from the Playground   58
Xiaomi's Low Price Strategy   59
Incheon International Airport: Offering Excitement   60
Not a Station, but a Platform   60
Success and Failure of Platform Strategy   62
Platform Evolution of 3M   62
Provide the Solution, Increase Satisfaction   62
Successful Innovation and Failed Improvement   64
Failure of Interplay: Pet.com   65
Why Pet.com Failed   65
Platforms in Transitional Periods: Social Commerce   66
The Profit Structure of Social Commerce   67
Social Commerce from the Platform Perspective   68

Part II   Platform as a Successful Business Strategy   71

Chapter 05   Characteristics of Successful Platform Strategy   73

Why Platform Strategy?   75
Modularization and the Rise of Platform Business   75
Closed, Converged Devices: The Case of IBM   75
From Vertical to Horizontal Structure   76
The Birth of Platform Strategy   77
The Evolution of Apple through Open Platform Strategy   77
Success with Support from the Market   78
Platform over Device   79
Paradigm for Interplay   79
Ecosystem Wars   79
Platform Leadership   80
In the Same Boat   81
Ecosystem Structures   81
Formula for a Successful Platform   84

Golden Rules for Platforms   85
1. The Playground Principle   85
2. The Rule of Externality   86
3. Conductor, not Controller   86
4. The Rule of Honey Bees   87
5. The Principle of Openness   87
6. The Rule of Killer Contents   88
7. The Principle of Community and Communication   88
8. Boundary Rules   89
9. The Rule of the Intermediary   90
10. The Rule of Serendipity   91

Chapter 06   Platform Strategy for Success   93

Let Them Come and Stay   95
Platform Formation and Maintenance   95
Strategies for Promoting Revisiting   95
Initial Trial Strategy   95
Promoting Strategy   96
Why Las Vegas is More Popular than the Great Wall
of China   96
Be a Conductor, not a Dominator   98
Sharing or Plundering   98
Conductor Strategy vs. Dominator Strategy   99
Conductor Strategy   100
Dominator Strategy   101
Value Creation and Sharing   102
Maximization of Value Creation   103
Survival through Sharing and Distribution   104
Understand the Nature of the Business   105
The Nature of the Business and Killer Contents   105
The Nature of the Business and Ecosystem Strategy   106
Chinese Take-out Service and the Delivery Ecosystem   107
EDLP Solution of Walmart and Merchandising
Ecosystem   107

Platform Architecture Design 108
ICE and SPICE Management Models 109
Manage Platform Boundaries 112
Develop Platform Strategy 113

Chapter 07   Platform Evolution and the Future of Platforms 115

How Will Platforms Evolve? 117
The Rise of Information Technology 117
Decreasing Knowledge Asymmetry 117
Sharing and Co-utilization of Property 118
Disappearing Barriers 119
Platform Openness 119
Large-Scale Collaboration Using Information Technologies 119
Open vs. Closed Platforms 120
Platform as an Open Ecosystem 121
Building Online Platforms 122
Search Engine-Based Platforms 122
Electronic Commerce-Based Platforms 123
Social Network Service-Based Platforms 123
Smart Phone-Based Platforms 123
The War among Online Platforms 124
The Inevitable Clash 124
Complications 124
Google Enters the SNS and Electronic
Commerce Industries 124
Naver Expands its Territory through Social
Network Services 125
Amazon Obtains a Search Engine 125
Social Network Services and Social Commerce 126
Smartphone-Based Platforms for All Areas 126

Epilogue 129
Bibliography 133

Part I

Why Platform Now?

Chapter 01

A New Business Model

- Using Platforms for Play
- Various Definitions of Platform
- Traditional Platforms
- Is a Department Store a Platform?
- Economic Perspectives on Platforms
- Platform: A New Business Model
- Insist on Piping or Transform into Platform?

Is it possible to create 300,000 new jobs and to make
$1 billion simply by drinking and dancing for 4 or
5 days? It sounds ridiculous, but it happens at
Rio Carnival. Including indirect income from broadcasting
rights and other sources, the Rio Carnival, which is the
world's largest carnival, generates $3.2 billion annually for
the Brazilian economy. The Carnival is a type of platform,
a playground where people have fun; it brings enormous
financial benefits. Let us examine the use of platforms for
fun and profit-making.

Using Platforms for Play

The platform is not only the interface connecting various business participants, but it is also the location of the transaction. Having a viable platform strategy creates new businesses by gathering many related businesses in one place. In the sense that it requires cooperation from many business actors, a platform strategy is opposite to a stand-alone strategy. For example, the Rio Carnival attracts tourists by offering new attractions in the parades every year through a competition among many Samba schools.

Platform strategy leaders create values and resolve issues when they interface with business partners. During this process, the platform becomes active, its members get more organized, and an ecosystem is created through the interface experience. A platform consists of a group of members in a business ecosystem in which members can play around. Using this definition, we can understand the offline platform as a physical space where people move around, and the online platform as a space in which content is located and software is utilized. A platform also consists of a platformer. The main role of the platformer is to provide a good business environment, a playground in which sellers, buyers, and community members can interact. Constant maintenance of the playground is also the responsibility of the platformer.

When serendipity occurs during the interface process, more people come to the platform. If a star is born there, the company that owns the playground also succeeds. This is the benefit of platform strategy. Good platform leadership is essential to the process of creating an industrial ecosystem where the active participation of all members produces profit. Platform leaders are responsible for supporting the health of an ecosystem that engages on their platform.

Platform strategy is utilized especially in the IT industry. The term "platform" in the IT industry refers to the hardware or software which forms the basis of the computer system on which people can develop various programs. For example, the main frame is the platform on which large-scale databases can be built, and operating systems such as Windows, UNIX, and LINUX are platforms where relevant software can be operated.

While it is true that the IT industry is the major industry in which the concept of platform is used, it is not the only one. Platform has played an important role during revolutionary times. Platforms at train stations built by George Stephenson at the beginning of the 19th century led to the Industrial Revolution. Also, Steve Jobs pioneered the Smart Revolution by creating platforms such as the iPod and iPhone.

The Smart Era has begun, and it encompasses far more than its predecessor, the Digital Era. Therefore, the significance of platform strategy is ever-increasing. Various platforms appropriated to the Smart Era must be developed. New IT platforms will accelerate the Smart Revolution, leading our society into this new era.

Various Definitions of Platform

Although many companies have declared themselves to be the platform of their industries or have claimed to be platform leaders in their fields, it seems difficult to get a clear definition of the word "platform". In fact, it may be impossible to have a conclusive definition with so many different perspectives on the meaning of "platform".

Major definitions of platform	
Meyer & Lehnerd (1997) Company Platform	A set of assets organized in a common structure from which a company can efficiently develop and produce a stream of derivative products
Gawer & Cusumano (2002) Industry Platform	Products, services, or technologies developed by one or more firms, and which serve as foundations upon which a larger number of firms can build further complementary innovations, in the form of specific products, related services, or component technologies
Iansiti & Levien (2004) A Set of Solutions	A set of solutions to problems that is made available to the members of the ecosystem through a set of access points and interfaces

(Continued)

(Continued)

Rochet & Tirole (2003) Two-sided Market (TSM)	Markets that "get both sides on board" by charging more to one set of customers in order to increase demand by others
Evans (2003) Two-sided Platform (TSP)	Businesses that create value by providing products that enable two or more different types of customers to get together, find each other, and exchange value
Haigu (2007) Multi-sided Platform (MSP)	An organization that creates value primarily by enabling direct interactions between two or more distinct types of affiliated customers

In this chapter, we examine some of the major definitions and their trends to improve our understanding of the platform.

Many companies use the word, "platform," as they develop new products through gradual innovations based on existing components or technologies. From this point of view, platform is defined as a subordinate system, an interface which, when combined as a common structure, makes efficient development and production possible. Such a platform is called a "product platform" or "inner platform". A company can respond to the needs of customers by combining components in new ways or by adding some components to previous combinations. A good platform strategy encompasses the development of a basic model that results in various products with some changes in component combinations.

A product platform has various advantages, including reduced costs, increased efficiency due to recycling the design and use of common parts, and flexibility in product design. Gawer and Cusumano (2002) and Iansiti and Levien (2004) expanded the concept of the product platform to the industrial context. They described how the basic components or technologies (solutions) from one company are made available to other companies, forming a community of participating companies that innovate based on this platform. The level of openness depends on the area. Accessibility of the interface information, freedom to utilize the platform, and the cost of the license and royalties determine the openness of the platform.

An industrial platform[1] expedites the innovation of complementary goods. As an example, Windows, which is the operating system of Microsoft, is a platform for which many complementary programs have been developed. As more complementary goods are developed through innovation, the value of the platform is strengthened along with its connection to its participants. As a result, as the platform grows, rivals or newcomers have more difficulty in disconnecting the participants from the platform. In addition, increased complementary goods becomes another barrier. One good example is that many people do not abandon the Windows operating system, even though other companies have developed excellent operating systems. Therefore, the downside of an industrial platform is that it often eliminates competition in the market.

The term "platform" has been used for two-sided markets or multi-sided markets. These economic terms are described as follows. Two-sided markets connect two groups benefiting from the network, and multi-sided markets connect more than two groups. In these markets, a company creates value by becoming or providing a platform where two or more customers can get together. Customers come to need one another in various ways, and they depend on the platform as an intermediary. Examples of two-sided markets include the credit card (card user and stores), computer operating systems (users and developers), phone directory (advertisers and customers), video games (gamers and game developers), job search websites (employers and job seekers), and search engines (advertisers and users).

The two-sided market has different characteristics from the merchant market. First, in the two-sided market, the platform offers interaction between two different groups. Secondly, the

---

[1] Operating systems such as Windows and Linux; microprocessors such as Intel or ARM; the iPod, iPhone, iPad, iOS, and App stores of Apple; Google's search engine and Android's operating system; SNS such as Facebook and Twitter; video game consoles; and various other goods and technologies all play roles in the industrial platform.

two-sided market allows two groups to have direct interplay. Thirdly, the two-sided market has indirect network effects (also called cross-network effects). As the number of participants increases, the value of the platform also increases. For example, store managers prefer to be affiliated with credit cards that have many users. Fourthly, the two-sided market has a unique pricing system. For example, to increase the size of the network, a certain group may be charged lower prices than the production cost, or they may be provided with a subsidy.

In this book, we examine the concept of the platform from the solution and two-sided market standpoints. The former emphasizes the approach to solutions, and the latter emphasizes the platform as a new market mechanism. These two standpoints differ in their emphasis on the value of the platform: either on the affiliated participants, or on the solutions it offers.

All businesses have customers or partners. The platform approach depends on how the business looks at them and what role the company chooses to take in the interplay between them. A business support organization or a student employment office at a college is a platform from the solution standpoint. In contrast, businesses offering a forum for interplay among customers, or an employment website are platforms from the two-sided market standpoint.

Traditional Platforms

The platform is not a new business model. Various types of platforms have been developed in the past. For instance, the newspaper is a platform connecting the reader and the advertiser, and the telephone directory is a platform connecting the user and the advertiser. Currency we use every day can also be understood as a platform connecting users and marketers. Among the various available currencies, the American dollar, the Euro, the Japanese Yen, and the British Pound are key global platforms (key currency).

Comparison of platform approaches

Solution Standpoints	Two-sided Market Standpoints
Product platform, industry platform, a group of solutions	Two-sided market, multi-sided market, multi-side platform
Interested in the development of attractive solutions	Interested in connections and matching
Implicit consideration of users	Clear inclusion of users
Better business ecosystem makes market successful	Connection platforms between sellers and buyers
All companies that provide solutions, e.g. Walmart, discount stores, franchises, Intel, global component companies	Newspaper, phone directory, matchmaker Credit card Airport, train station, subway station, bus terminal
Meyer & Lehnerd (1997) Gawer & Cusumano (2002) Iansiti & Levien (2004)	Rochet & Tirole (2003) Evans (2003), Haigu (2007)

Credit Card

A credit card is a payment platform which connects card holders and affiliated stores. For example, the Visa card exclusively connects Visa card owners and Visa card-affiliated stores. Therefore, the first focus for the Visa Company is membership, both for card holders and stores.

In a traditional market, every buyer has equal worth. However, a credit card is not worthwhile unless its membership exceeds a certain threshold. In economics terms, we talk about economies of scale. Consumers like credit cards that have many member stores, and stores prefer to accept cards that have many users. Credit card companies spend a lot of money in attracting new members and in providing various, optional services, because nearly half of their profits are generated from fees.

Newspapers

Among newspapers, we often notice a fierce competition to acquire readers by giving away all kinds of gifts. This competition occurs, because the newspaper is a platform. It differs from the credit card in that its potential readers rarely consider the number of subscribers or advertisers in their choice of newspaper. On the other hand, advertisers consider which newspaper has the largest number of readers, because they are interested in obtaining the widest possible effects of the advertisement. Therefore, newspapers take considerable pains to increase their readership.

Newspapers are often distributed free on the street. In the newspaper business, free distribution is a common way to increase readership. With free distribution, newspaper companies can claim that they have a large share of the market. No one talks about the Fair Trade Act regarding this practice, and the newspaper companies get more than enough compensation from the practice through advertisements. However, since the newspaper rating system started counting only regular paying subscribers, competition for subscribers has intensified, and all kinds of incentive programs have been initiated.

Free newspaper distribution has almost disappeared, as readers have started depending on their smartphones for their news. Newspaper platforms are being replaced by the new online platforms.

Video Games

Buyers of game consoles want to have fun and excitement through playing games. Game developers want to create games for popular game consoles (platforms). To make a game platform successful, a minimum number of games must be developed, and a sufficient number of users must play the game.

Big video game platforms such as Sony, Sega, and Nintendo have sources of profit other than the sales of game consoles. Their major profits come from royalties for use of their gaming platforms. Even when video game consoles are sold at less than the cost of production, these consoles become loss leaders. When users buy more consoles, a virtuous cycle develops in which users bring along developers, which continue to bring along users. The cycle continues as some of those new users seek to purchase new consoles. However, there have been many cases of failed game platforms despite excellent technologies.

When a technology is too sophisticated, it becomes difficult to develop good quality games for it. This is why Microsoft chose the x86 and Windows platforms, which were familiar to game developers when the Xbox was launched in 2001.

In the video game industry, the key competitive elements are the price and the ease of use of the operating system. It is a different story when it comes to online or mobile games. First of all, game consoles are replaced by the platforms and operating systems of computers and smartphones. Even social network services (SNS) like WhatsApp act as platforms since users play games on them. This situation has changed the source of profit for game developers to advertisement or sales of game-related items.

Matchmaking Business

According to the Matrimonial Brokerage Management Act, match-making refers to counseling and arrangement for the purpose of marriage. Matchmakers earn their income from commission, fees, and other sources. About 1,500 matchmaking companies operate actively in Korea; among these, 4 or 5 big companies are leading the market, which is estimated to be around 150 million USD, according to the statistics at the end of 2019.

The matchmaking business can be considered as a platform which connects two different groups of men and women. Therefore, as we observed in the case of credit cards, newspapers, and video games, this platform becomes more attractive as the number of users increases. For instance, when a woman selects a matchmaking company, she may prefer a company with a large number of male members. Therefore, companies with a large number of male members will attract a greater number of female members, after which it will attract more men. The result is a virtuous cycle.

The ultimate purpose of a matchmaking company is marriage for its members. Therefore, matchmaking services require a balanced number of male and female members and a swift matching mecha-nism. Even if the matchmaking platform has a large pool of members, if the gender balance in its membership is not well maintained, business success is not guaranteed.

Is a Department Store a Platform?

A shopping mall, which has several stores in one building, is a typical platform. The more stores it has, and the more shoppers come to the building, the higher the value of the shopping mall. The question then arises, what about the department store? Is it a platform or not?

Unlike the department stores in the U.S or the U.K., which use the direct purchase method, Korean department stores utilize the specified purchase method.[2] In Korea, 90% of department stores use the specified purchase method, and 90% of discount stores utilize the direct purchase method. Unlike in other countries, Korean department stores are not "retailers" which purchase goods and sell them to consumers. Rather, a Korean department store is a "rental business" which allows independent brands to open their shops in the building, taking a certain percentage of the sales as commission. Therefore, enterprises that have set up shop in the department store are basically tenants. From this perspective, we may conclude that department stores in Korea are platforms, not resellers.

The Department Store as a Solution

Department stores in Korea provide solutions for both business enterprises and shoppers. They provide the shopper with entertainment and various modes of consumption, and the enterprises operating within the store with reliability and a stable source of sales. Department stores also give to the stores opportunities to contact many customers, thereby reducing uncertainty. At the same time, due to the brand

---

[2] A method in which the department store purchases goods, but pays the supplier after the goods are sold. In this method, the department stores also charge a certain amount of commission to their suppliers. Also, they need not worry about inventory clearance.

Platform elements of department stores

Distinction	Contents
Hardware	Buildings, parking lots, rest areas, land
Software	Development of merchandising and complimentary goods
	Personal service from salespeople, card services, customer relationship management, delivery services
	Cultural and entertainment areas, food court
	Brand image, public relations, advertisement

value of the department store, business enterprises situated within it can increase the credibility of their own brands. Another benefit of opening a shop in a department store is that it is economical in terms of investment and maintenance costs, compared with having an independent store.

At a department store, shoppers get the benefit of convenience, as they can do various kinds of shopping in one place. In addition, they can enjoy the diverse experiences of dining, cultural events, and educational programs. In Korean department stores, the food and beverage services play a particularly important role in attracting customers (i.e., the food court, restaurants, and grocery corners) because many people come to a department store to enjoy good foods.

The Department Store as a Two-Sided Market

From the market point of view, department stores act as platforms for two-sided markets, connecting the shops and the shoppers. Department stores in Korea have many characteristics of shopping malls. Rather than making profit from reselling goods purchased externally, they make profit from commissions. There are certain sections in department stores that employ the direct purchase system, like the food market and some private brand shops. However, the main profit comes from the rent and commission they received from the shops. In this sense, it is a similar system to that of a shopping mall.

For example, if a customer who needs a suit comes to a department store in Korea, he goes to a shop which is a tenant in the building. In fact, the customer buys a suit from the shop, not from the department store. If the customer pays one million won, the money goes into the account of the department store first, after which the department store gives 660,000 won back to the shop. The department store owes the shop this amount, since it takes a commission of 34% of one million won. According to the report of the Korean Fair Trade Commission in 2014, the average department store commission rate is 28% (shirts and ties 33.8%, children's items 31.9%, leisure items 31.5%, books and music 13.7%, and digital items 14.2%).

The department store makes various efforts to increase its competitiveness as a platform. The first priorities are location and merchandising. The entertainment and food sections are also major foci. Recently, as the gap between the wealthy and the poor is increasing, and shopping patterns are changing accordingly, Korean department stores have made special efforts to attract VIP customers. While they have paid attention to the shopper side of the market, department stores have been less attentive toward shops. Different commission rates apply to the shops depending on the type of items they sell, their contribution to the store, and the value of the brand. Shops that do not match their sales goals may be evicted.

Because of our familiarity with the platform known as the department store, we tend to think of it as different from eBay, Google, Android, and iPhone. However, there is no difference between the department store and these IT-based platforms in the sense that all are connection chains.

Economic Perspectives on Platforms

Professor Jean Tirole, the Nobel Laureate in 2014, is a pioneer in the field of platform economics. The term "platform market", which is also called the two-sided market, means a market which connects more than two participants who benefit from its existence. Examples include video game consoles, credit cards, newspapers, shopping malls, and Google. One of the main characteristics of these platform markets is that participants on both sides have influence on each other's demands. In order to operate a video game platform, a sufficient number of games should be developed, and enough people have to use it. Advertisers are interested in how many subscribers a newspaper has as a measure of the effectiveness of advertisement in this medium.

This reciprocity in the platform market causes a problem: the price a platform imposes on one side influences the demands of the other side. For example, if credit card membership fees are expensive and there is no additional benefit from using that card, it is difficult to increase the number of users. In turn, the number of member stores will not increase. Alternatively, if the credit card fees for the stores are too expensive, very few stores will accept that card, and people will not want to use it.

When one side of the market is harder to attract than the other side, the platform determines the price for maximum profit. Sometimes subsidies are offered. Good examples include the case when a newspaper company charges less than the cost of production to its subscribers, or Microsoft sells the Xbox at the same or a lower price than its production costs. Its profits come from selling publishing rights to game developers or earning royalties from game sales. One final example: Google allows one side (users) to use its search engine for free while accepting payment from the other side (advertisers).

Professor Jean Tirole discusses what determines how much a platform charges its participants. The simplest business situation is the merchant market. In this case, demand is determined by the amount the company charges. However, the platform market is two-sided. Apple sells its customers iPhones, taking 30% of App sales. In this case, how much Apple charges for the iPhone, the price of Apps, and other associated fees all determine the demand for iPhones and their Apps. In short, these two markets are connected.

The problem is simple if the platform sets a price for profit maximization in each market separately. However, the two-sided market is not that simple. The number of people who own iPhones is a significant determinant of how much an App developer invests in developing new iPhone Apps. In turn, the number of Apps consumers can use with the iPhone is a significant factor in their choice to buy the phone. It makes sense that companies reduce prices if they can increase demand by giving up some profit from one side or the other.

Professor Tirole also shows how the power or price of a platform influences the market. Traditionally in most countries, the practice of dumping has been restricted by the Fair Trade Act. When a company sells its products at a price lower than the production costs, it eliminates competitors. This is an effective practice for a company to eliminate competitors and to gain control over the market. Once the company gains control over the market, it will increase the price to recover the cost for dumping.

However, dumping works differently in the platform market. Newspaper companies distribute newspapers for free, not because they want to eliminate their competitors, but because they want to gain more revenue from advertisers by attracting more subscribers. In this case, dumping should perhaps not be restricted.

Applying the principle of the platform market, the best price is not always at the point where marginal costs and marginal profits meet. In the platform market, the price should be determined by considering how much it improves the well-being of the market as a whole.

Platform: A New Business Model

Platform strategy is different from traditional business strategy. The traditional business model is that the company produces goods and sells them. The platform business model, on the other hand, is that the company enlarges itself by improving the business ecosystem. The traditional business model focuses on the short-term pursuit of profit using a production and merchandising model. By contrast, the platform is a long-term business model focused on creating an attractive ecosystem and evolving within it.

The platform creates a playground, builds a market, and offers participants solutions in order to increase its user base. These solutions are often called the "invisible engine" of the platform, or the "killer contents". However, if the solution does not provide the participants with enough value, the platform loses its attractiveness. In addition, serendipity, or unexpected fun should be provided along with solutions in order to attract more users.

For example, Apple's iPhone provides a platform and an interface. Unlike companies that provide limited applications from suppliers, Apple provides a platform on which anyone can create App products. In addition, Apple created the App market, which had 300,000 participants within 30 months, and became the market leader. Apple grew fast in a short period of time because of the explosive expansion of the creative ecosystem of App developers based on the iPhone platform. This ecosystem provided solutions and serendipity to its users.

Apple was not complacent with this success, however; it expanded its business ecosystem through the development of an MP3 player, a music provider, and a docking audio system based on the iPhone. It also maximized value by reinforcing the interface and developing connecting software and hardware such as iTunes, the App Store, and the iPad.

Apple is an excellent example of how a company can succeed using the platform strategy. By creating a platform and focusing on its maintenance to provide a group interface on the playground, Apple became the leading company in its industry. It continues to expand the ecosystem with the development of other products, which will facilitate the evolution of the business.

Insist on Piping or Transform into Platform?

To understand what platform strategy is, we examine very different, existing business strategies. The concepts of openness, sharing, collaboration, and ecosystem, which are emphasized in platform strategy, are absent from what we in this book call "piping strategy".

Piping strategy entails the establishment of a network of pipes with a well-planned structural design. Traditional manufacturing companies in the 1970s are good examples. With this strategy, several essential things are planned ahead: how value will be created, and how products and services will reach customers through what kind of process. After planning, the company builds an infrastructure, and all business activities conform to this well-structured plan. This sticking to the well-structured plan is a fundamental difference between piping strategy and platform strategy. Platform strategy allows participants to collaborate with each other to redesign and develop new structures within the ecosystem, and all business activities contribute to the evolution of the ecosystem.

Another difference is that the plan developed through the piping strategy is exclusive. It is closed. Any attempt to change the plan without permission is like a criminal act, which is absolutely prohibited. In the traditional business model, if someone without a permit reprocesses the data, tries to reproduce the parts or products, or provides related or similar services, swift repercussions follow. By contrast, the platform encourages these behaviors.

In piping strategy, expansion of or changes in the network of pipes must happen under the control of the company based on its original plan. However, in platform strategy, any participant can expand or change the platform because the process of changes is a natural part of the evolution of the platform.

In the past, most businesses adopted the piping strategy not because they wanted to, but because they lacked understanding of platform strategy and because the piping model was more appropriate at the time. In the business environment of the past, planning and structuring was best executed by single companies alone. At the time, few technologies and resources were available, and the possibility of incorporating outsiders into the business was quite low. Even if it was possible, their contribution was quite limited. In addition, there was no appropriate means to monitor participants' activities to ensure the best business outcomes. These conditions led to the conclusion that it was more efficient for a capable company to establish its own infrastructure, allowing other companies to join in only as suppliers or subcontractors. Under these circumstances, participating companies could only execute the job demanded of them by the leading company.

Circumstances have changed. In certain areas, individuals and small businesses have knowledge and capability similar to and competitive with those of large companies. Moreover, effective communication technology is available to facilitate smooth collaboration with outside participants. In this environment, it is more efficient to do business by inviting all available talents, both internal and external, to the company rather than doing everything alone. This is why the platform has appeared and why platform strategy has gradually replaced piping strategy.

Of course, not all businesses operating on the existing piping model will adopt platform strategy. Depending on the field and industry, piping can sometimes be a more appropriate model even in this new era. However, the reality is that the piping model will be replaced by the platform model more and more as time passes. As business people, we must therefore ask ourselves, in this changing business environment, whether we will stick to the piping model or change over to the platform model.

Chapter 02

Platform Operation and the Open Ecosystem

- Operation of the Platform
- Platform Ecosystems

Platforms produce ecosystems with various elements and participants, and as a result of their activities, ecosystems changed and evolved. Platform ecosystems emphasize collaboration rather than competition. In addition, platformers prefer leaving the door open rather than closed. In a platform ecosystem, sustainable development is achieved through openness and cooperation. In this chapter, we examine the principles on which the platform ecosystem operates.

Operation of the Platform

Platform Composition

Platforms have many different structures, depending on the field, but there are some common elements. They can be classified into three groups. The first is hardware and associated devices, through which value is transmitted. The second is the contents, or the actual reason for having the platform. Finally, there is the interface through which hardware and software solutions are realized. The following table displays these elements.

For example, the airport is a platform providing customers with the value of traveling. It requires the hardware of airplanes and an airport terminal. In addition, it requires services from employees for ticketing and check-ins. These are the contents of the airport. The business ecosystem of the airport includes travel agencies, airline companies, immigration offices, security desks, and duty-free shops. Each participant here adds different value to the platform.

Elements of platforms

Elements	Definition	Train Station, Airport	iTunes	Amazon	Facebook
Hardware and Devices	The physical infra-structure through which value is transmitted	Train, airplane, railway station, airport terminal	System through which music and apps can be stored and utilized on iPhone, iPod, iPad	Shopping and delivery system involving a catalog and computer or smart phone	System used to store, analyze, and utilize the social information of users
Contents	Immaterial software, contents, and system operating the device	Service and manage-ment activities (e.g., ticketing, check-in)	Apps, music	Product and customer rating inform-ation	Photos, documents, and other social information shared among users

(Continued)

(*Continued*)

Elements	Definition	Train Station, Airport	iTunes	Amazon	Facebook
Interface	Space or means through which interaction between objects and users is accomplished	Railway, airport shuttle, runway	iOS	Internet, Apps	Internet, Apps

iTunes offers various kinds of information and entertainment through devices such as the iPhone, the iPod, and the iPad. To provide value, various app developers, telecom companies, and online advertisers join the iTunes platform, which is composed of hardware as well as software.

Amazon established a platform called the online shopping mall on the internet. It provided products at low costs and at customers' convenience. Companies participating on this platform include the sellers, FedEx, and UPS.

Facebook built a platform to connect people with one another through computers and smartphones. Its values include connectivity and information provision for users. Many telecommunications, gaming, and software development companies are participants on this platform, providing supplementary services.

The Roles of Platform Participants

Platform participants are entities and individuals that comprise the business ecosystem around the platform. These individual participants of a platform business ecosystem can be classified by their roles. First, there is the platformer, who is the creator of the platform.

Then, there are evangelists and complementors. These participants produce the next generations of the ecosystem by pollination and furthering its evolution. In the industrial ecosystem, the company that owns the platform (the platformer) organizes the ecosystem. At the same time, the platformer often takes on the role of evangelist, connecting small businesses (the complementors) to one another in the ecosystem.

A platform prospers as more small businesses get together to occupy the platform. Complementors that increase the attractiveness of the platform may include app developers or venture businesses. Their focus and efforts toward technological innovation through research and development create a sustainable ecosystem and contribute to its evolution. Before analyzing platform strategy, we first examine platform participants and their roles in a healthy industrial ecosystem.

Among these platform participants, the most significant is the platformer. However, the platformer does not dominate or reign over others, but acts as a conductor who serves the platform. The platformer produces the killer contents or solutions. In addition, it facilitates activities in the market, with its killer contents, by providing or organizing serendipity. The degree to which it excites the participants is the key to the success of the platform.

Major platform participants

Participants	Role in the Ecosystem	Responsibilities
Platformer	Organizer of the ecosystem	Plan and organize the ecosystem, coordinate its devices and contents, and execute service provision.
Evangelists	Business app scouters	Diplomatic external relations, leading the growth of the ecosystem by bringing partners onto the platform.
Complementors	Program providers and app developers	Develop complementary products and services for the platform, adding value to the existing platform as a niche player

Platform Ecosystems

The Crisis of Business Education

Many CEOs have graduated from liberal arts schools instead of business school. This reveals a problem in business administration education. What is the problem?

First, in business education, the focus on "people" is missing. By contrast, Liberal Arts programs teach various ways to understand human behavior. To overcome this crisis in business education, we need to take a new approach.

In his 4 P strategy (product, price, place, promotion), Professor Emeritus Philip Kotler asserts that the program at the Kellogg Business School lacks the "people" element. The business administration program at his school emphasizes the system of rules and incentives for execution of competitive strategy. Because it looks at human behavior only from a functional perspective, it values the success of the system more than the human element. From this point of view, the company becomes the lord, and the humans serve as slaves.

The programs of business administration in existence today do not allow for the happiness of the members of the company. It is true that the system is important for a successful outcome in the short-term and protects the company from the "worst-case scenario," but excessive emphasis on regulations will minimize creativity and lead to various side effects. Therefore, business administration programs should focus on how the members of the company can gain healthy ownership of their work.

Secondly, existing business strategies emphasize the "I" rather than the "we". This problem is more apparent in the theory of competition strategy, in which companies are driven out to the battlefield. This theory is based on the single-sided market model.

Companies in the single-sided market risk their survival to produce good products. To them, product innovation is all-important in the battle of devices. In this battle, everybody is the "enemy". In short, competition strategy is a "stand-alone", survival strategy in which companies must survive by ultimately eliminating all competitors. The stand-alone strategy produces a small number of winners and a majority of losers. This leads to the polarization of society and causes social problems such as those that led to "Occupy Wall Street!"

Thirdly, business administration programs focus on short-term management. Such short-sighted micro-management focuses on a particular aspect of business. It may be effective in the short-term, but not in the long history of the company. All companies must co-exist in their relations with other organizations within the business ecosystem.

The alternative suggested by these critics of the business administration programs is to approach business problems from the ecosystem perspective. The ecosystem is the place where various industrial organisms live together. In the ecosystem, these organisms influence one another and interact with the environment. In the ecosystem, cooperative interaction rather than competition is important. Business administration programs will survive best by evolving along with the market and emphasizing cooperation rather than competition.

No More Competition

As Information Technology (IT) continues to bring out new innovations, competition among global business ecosystems has been intensified. For example, the business ecosystems of Apple and Google have been evolving. They have been focusing not on the battle of devices, but the battle of platforms. In addition to iTunes for the iPod and the App Store for the iPhone, they have recently added the voice recognition and AI ecosystems.

The iPhone includes a voice recognition program, called Siri, that was developed by Dag Kittlaus. This voice recognition program has created a new interface ecosystem. The voice is the most convenient interface. What made this possible is that a platformer understood the potential of Siri as an interface within its platform.

Platform strategy, based on the industrial ecosystem business model, tends to bring out heroes who lead the battles of the ecosystem. Large companies must make innovative small businesses its heroes and learn how to develop a healthy ecosystem within them, where everybody can prosper. This is the symbiotic development model.

Business management strategy has long been based on traditional concepts of economics, in which the importance of unlimited competition is emphasized. Nowadays, we understand business management in terms of the organic structure of the market and how synergy created from the coexistence of various businesses becomes the foundation of economic competitiveness on the national level.

The traditional concepts of business management are based on the unlimited competition of human selfishness. In the past, it was believed that competition creates competitiveness. A new concept of business management appeared when James Moore published "The End of Competition" in 1996. Moore looked at business management from a biological viewpoint with understanding of the ecosystem, focusing on the coexistence and evolution of businesses. Symbiotic development in the marketplace emphasizes fair competition and cooperative relations, which create economic synergy. Cooperative relations between a large company and its suppliers are viewed as the foundation of business and as a new means of gaining a competitive edge.

Welcome Everybody

The success of a company depends not only on the capability of the company itself, but also on the success of the industrial ecosystem. Even if a large company has a good platform, it cannot succeed if its complementors, such as application developers and suppliers do not cooperate. In the same way, the success of each individual complementor largely depends on the ability and output of other complementors or suppliers.

In nature, the fate of a species is shared with the fate of the ecosystem to which it belongs. Like this principle of nature, the business ecosystem can be healthy only when its individual business organisms are healthy. When individual organisms are healthy, we can expect synergic effects in the whole ecosystem. By contrast, one weak spot in the ecosystem can diminish the outcomes for all.

The business ecosystem is not a static world in which one participant leads the others, but a dynamic world where various participants engage in constant interplay, and evolution occurs. What it considers important is the symbiotic value chains among species, the birth of new species, and the evolution of the ecosystem. In other words, to carry the biological analogy further, it is interested in the breeding of and the expansion of the ecosystem.

Competition is less important than the symbiotic relations here. Flowers and bees have a symbiotic relationship. Without pollination by bees, flowers cannot produce fruit. When many bees visit the flowers, the flowers can produce fruit, and the cycle of life will continue. This is the healthy regeneration of an ecosystem in nature.

The success of Apple's iPod and iPhone came from the fact that the company changed the walled garden into an open garden. Apple succeeded due to the symbiotic relations with its affiliated companies or complementors. It created a healthy ecosystem by sharing profits with these affiliated companies. This platform strategy led its contents ecosystem to prosper.[1]

The Software in the End

For a number of years, the Korean television programs, "Superstar K" and "K-pop Star", captivated the attention of an entire nation. What was the driving reason behind this phenomenon? These two, talent audition series transformed a closed ecosystem into an open ecosystem. Each time the curtain went up, the relatively unknown performers would come forward and provide unpredictable entertainment to audiences who were tired of the limited options that were previously available to them (performers who had already achieved success & fame).

---

[1] iPhone is not a totally open platform, although it is more open than before. This will be explained later in the case studies of companies that have successfully implemented platform strategy.

According to Professor Andrei Hagiu of Harvard University, platform strategy involves simultaneously creating an ecosystem and overcoming the traditional framework of corporate domination over competitors. Therefore, a company implementing platform strategy must resemble a flower attracting bees and butterflies in order to create the ecosystem. As creator of the ecosystem, the company must hire a CEO to be an architect or a program director, someone who can excite people and bring important players into the ecosystem.

"To excite people" was the primary goal of the producers of "Superstar K" and "K-pop Star", while "to invent the app ecosystem" was the brainchild of Steve Jobs. These people were directors, not dictators. As a result of Jobs' efforts, Apple succeeded in creating the app ecosystem, in which multitudes of people are engaged.

Google acquired Motorola, and Microsoft bought Nokia's mobile business division.[2] They thereby transformed themselves into smartphone manufacturers, preparing for battle with Apple, the current market leader. At the same time, creators in the contents market are developing the open ecosystem through cloud computing.

When Microsoft acquired Nokia, it ceased all cooperation with strategic manufacturing partners such as Samsung. Thereafter, the two companies entered into a competitive relationship. This change had a serious impact on the manufacturing industrial ecosystem in Korea. The fear was this: If Apple, Google, and Microsoft closed the platform related to the operating system, Samsung and LG would lose their smartphone operating system. As a result, the smartphone industry's ecosystem in Korea would be threatened.

The smart era is the software era. What makes the smartphone smart depends on the competitive edge provided by software. In short, the smart revolution is a software revolution. Hence, success in the smart era requires a sufficient supply of talent within the software industry.

---

[2] Both Google and Microsoft ended up selling their smartphone businesses. It was because they could not compete with ecosystems, such as iOS and Android, as individual companies.

The Ecosystem Approach

Mao Zedong: Lessons from the Four Pests Campaign

In the fall, people place scarecrows in their rice paddies to prevent sparrows from eating their grains and ruining their harvest. So, are sparrows the enemies of the rice harvest?

In 1958, Mao Zedong started the "Great Leap Forward Movement" and "Four Pests Campaign". The Great Leap Forward Movement was intended to accelerate economic growth of China through increased production. The focus of this movement was an increase in the rice production rate. Also, for this purpose, Mao Zedong started the Four Pests Campaign. The four pests were sparrows, mosquitoes, flies, and rats. The Four Pests Campaign involved the killing of these pests.

Among these pests, the one that damaged the rice harvest most was the sparrows. The farmers submitted a petition about the harm to crops caused by sparrows. Therefore, the Chinese government set out to improve its rice harvest by killing all the sparrows (Kim, Myung-Ho: *The Story of the Chinese People: the Memory of Sparrow Killings*).

In 1958, the Chinese government established a bureau for the extermination of sparrows in Beijing and started a war on sparrows. Sticks, slingshots, and poison cookies were prepared, after which a large parade was held celebrating the extermination of the sparrows. As a result, over two thousand million sparrows were killed. This cull nearly annihilated the total sparrow population.

Did this campaign result in a successful rice harvest? No. As sparrows disappeared, as of 1959, the number of insects in China increased. In 1960, an attack of locusts caused half of the expected rice harvest to disappear. As a result, 40 million people died of starvation.

The failure of the Great Leap Forward Movement made Mao Zedong resign from the position of Premier. The importance of sparrows to the ecosystem was recognized, and the Chinese government imported two hundred thousand sparrows from the Soviet Union.

Let us go back to the question. Are sparrows the enemies of the rice harvest? No. The enemies were people obsessed with a short-term goal. War or competition may be effective in accomplishing short-term goals. However, in the long run, they are harmful to health and sustainability.

Chapter 03

Two Pillars of Value Creation
by the Platform

- Everybody Shares
- Hand in Hand
- Cross-Network Value

The success of a platform business depends on how many businesses or people are connected and cooperate through the platform. One of the important reasons why a platform appears in the market is that the infrastructure it offers produces value for participants and allows them to obtain synergy from cooperation.

The platform's architecture or governance, which are considered significant elements, facilitate interplay among participants and promote repeated use. The two pillars of value creation of the platform are economies of scale and network effect (or network externalities).

Everybody Shares

Economies of scale is a basic concept in economics. Let us examine a case of platform strategy in the car industry. With a platform based on a basic design, an automobile company can develop many lines of cars. Here, the company can reduce the cost of developing new designs for every line of car that they produce, because the basic design is shared across product lines.

Outsourcing is another example of economies of scale. Outsourcing companies can save on operating costs in the service they provide to other companies, since they can take advantage of their existing infrastructure for current clients. In that way, they can provide their clients with services at lower prices. As a result, their customers also benefit from working with the outsourcing company.

In the case of Amazon, when sellers use Amazon's services, they are paying off what the company spent developing its infrastructure. Since the sellers share these fixed costs initially paid by Amazon, as more sellers use Amazon, prices for each seller are reduced over time. This is the effect of economies of scale.

Therefore, to maximize the benefits of economies of scale, Amazon attempts to attract more customers. Especially in cases where the variable costs of the infrastructure are low or nil, doing business becomes more profitable as the number of customers increases, since the only costs they have to pay are fixed. This is particularly apparent in the case of digital platforms such as Amazon or Apple's App Store. These platforms have very low variable costs regardless of the number of customers. As a result, they gain more benefits as the company attracts more customers.

One of the typical platforms pursuing value creation through the economies of scale is the outsourcing business. Nowadays, many companies hire contractors for IT, human resources, and marketing purposes. The opposite of this outsourcing practice is insourcing, in which the company handles all aspects of business operations internally. In the past, many companies had their own IT departments, and all IT services necessary for running the business were provided within the company. However, more and more companies nowadays are hiring contractors for IT services. They are outsourcing the services they need to run their businesses. They use telecom companies to install infrastructure such as internet services and develop their systems with the aid of system developing companies. They also bring in companies that handle data collection and management.

There are many reasons for a company to hire a contractor, but the most common reason is cost reduction. Contractors typically provide their services at lower costs than it would cost for the company to handle the job itself. How can contractors provide services at lower costs? Let us look into the case of call centers, which many companies use these days. If a certain bank hires a call center service provider, that service provider has probably been hired by other banks, too. Naturally, the size of the call center increases as the number of customer banks increases. Eventually, the number of employees at the center may grow to 3,000 instead of 300, the number at which it started. Unit costs are lower for larger companies, because contractors enjoy economies of scale in terms of system development and management, employee training, and so on.

By the definition used in this study, an outsourcing service is a sort of platform. Outsourcing service companies have the hardware and software necessary to provide services. with the contents that customers are interested in. These outsourcing companies create more value by reducing unit costs for the service as the number of customers grows.

As the outsourcing service platform grows, ecosystem participants benefit from the improved infrastructure. However, the major benefit of an outsourcing platform is cost reduction in terms of economies of scale, rather than the interplay and connection between participants.

Hand in Hand

Facebook and WhatsApp are typical examples of how the value of a network itself increases the value of the platform. We can communicate with friends through WhatsApp instantly. Through Facebook, we can check how people we are interested in are doing, and let them know how we are doing. As previously mentioned, connectivity among people (i.e., the social network) is the major value of the platform.

These services also bring the benefit of economies of scale as they attract more users. From the point of view of a platformer who is operating a social network service, the unit cost for system management for each user diminishes as the number of users increases. However, if the number of users exceeds a certain limit, the benefits from economies of scale become less significant. Thus, social network companies try to attract more users not for economies of scale, but for the value of the network itself. The value of the network, which increases as more people use the service, is far more important for these companies than the effect of economies of scale.

Users are not interested in reducing costs for the social network service. Social network services are typically free; the companies make profits from advertisement or other sources of income. Therefore, cost is not a consideration when a user chooses social network services.

Services with strong externality (value creation from interactions), such as those providing social networks, increase their value exponentially as the number of users grows. This phenomenon is called "network effect". Potential users choose networks that have more users, so the competition among these companies for new users is fierce— truly a matter of survival. In this platform, the interplay among users has overwhelming power over the cost of the network.

The two axes of value creation for a platform can be understood using the graph below. There are cases where the economies of scale play a larger role depending on the type of platform, and also cases in which network effect plays the larger role. Of course, value creation by means of a platform requires more than two axes, but these two axes are the major ones behind creation of a platform and how the platform gets its value.

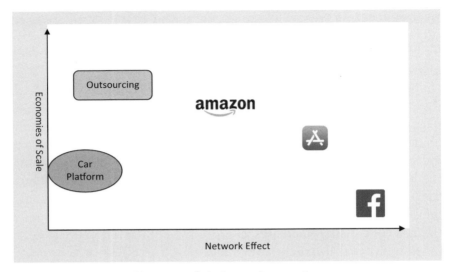

Two axes of platform value creation

Cross-Network Value

The network value of a platform is different from the general value of the network. If there are more phone owners or social network members, the value of the network increases. This is the general concept of network effect. Thinking about the example of the credit card, however, consumers may not think that a Visa card is better than other cards just because the number of cardholders increases. For a Visa card to be valuable, many stores must accept it. Consumers evaluate the value of a Visa card based on the number of member stores. For their part, stores evaluate the value of the Visa card based on the number of consumers using it. This is the "cross-network value" or "cross-network externality", in which both sides of the network find the value of the network from the numbers of the other side. The network effect of a business platform is enhanced by this cross-network value.

In the beginning stages of a platform business, the chicken and egg problem arise. The platform needs many sellers (e.g., apps, credit card member stores) to attract buyers (smartphone owners, credit card users). The problem is that sellers want to join a platform with many buyers. Platformers must decide whom to attract first, the buyers or the sellers. Ultimately, they are interested in the co-evolution of both sides of the market (Caillaud and Jullien, 2003; Eisenmann *et al.*, 2006).

Chapter 04

Successful Companies with Platform Businesses

- Companies with Platforms on the Internet
- Companies with Offline Platforms
- The Evolution of Collaboration: Open Innovation
- Platform Strategy for the Latecomer: Xiaomi
- Incheon International Airport: Offering Excitement
- Success and Failure of Platform Strategy

The platform takes a variety of modes in various industries. A platform and its many affiliates in the ecosystem are mutually influential. In this chapter, we examine some cases of successful platforms, while identifying the components of a platform and the key to its success.

Companies with Platforms on the Internet

Pioneer of the Mobile Platform: The Apple App Store

Apple's App Store is a famous example of a platform business. The App Store supports external contents developers, distributing and selling their contents. From the viewpoint of consumers, it plays the role of a platform where they can purchase the digital contents they need.

The App Store is unique in one respect. Application developers have to obtain permission from Apple before they list their products in the App Store. Therefore, it is not exactly an open platform.

Apple must have decided to take the middle road in resolving the dilemma between quality and quantity of contents. The closed policy of allowing only a small number of affiliated developers to participate would not have led to the rich contents we see on the App Store today. On the other hand, the totally open policy in which anybody can list products in the store would have left consumers unsatisfied with the low quality of contents, and they would eventually have left the store, abandoning the platform.

Destroying Borders: Facebook Connect

Facebook has been very successful as a social network platform. One of the main reasons for its success is that it provides external developers with a platform where they can situate various kinds of social network software. Website developers can take advantage of the platform functions of Facebook just by adding their own code. For example, the "Like" button on many websites makes use of the platform that Facebook provides.

Facebook Connect is the most important platform for Facebook technologically and strategically. Facebook Connect allows users to not only access Facebook functions, but it also provides access to external sites through their Facebook account ("Sign up with Facebook"). For example, we can see who among our Facebook friends have viewed certain products on certain sites. At the same time, managers of other websites can identify who among their customers' Facebook friends have visited their sites.

This function is so innovative and significant, because it destroys the border between Facebook and external sites. Therefore, Facebook Connect is beneficial to both Facebook and external sites. Facebook users can easily sign-in to other websites with one-click, while using a Facebook account, eliminating the need to repeatedly log-in their personal information. Furthermore, their activities on the external sites can be shared with other users through the Facebook News Feed. This amazing integration ultimately, serves to build trust between Facebook users and the external sites.

Facebook Connect is a brilliant innovation that has made advertisement and marketing possible through the utilization of a customer's social network. From the viewpoint of Facebook, it has all the advantages that come with a platform in that it can expand its network to almost all websites.

Open Platforms in Electronic Commerce

Open platforms are particularly useful in the world of electronic commerce. Having more users at an electronic commerce platform benefits both sellers and buyers. For sellers such as the App Store and Amazon, all platform users are potential buyers. Therefore, as the number of platform users grows, the benefit for sellers increases. In addition, buyers have the advantage of obtaining various kinds of products at lower prices as the platform increases in popularity. As more sellers join the network, competition among them benefits the buyers. Even with social networks such as Facebook, the open platform is preferable because value is created when more people utilize the service.

To have an efficient open platform in electronic commerce, all technological and systematic complementors have to perform their functions well. These complementors include search tools for products and contents, payment systems, quality assurance, and fraud protection. This is the PASS1 (platform as a set of solutions) strategy in electronic commerce.

There are three points to be considered in the matter of open platforms in electronic commerce. First, organization of the ideal platform means that the platformer does not control every aspect of commercial activity, but that many participants (individuals and small businesses) help build the base for profit creation. The platformer makes profit indirectly, while participants create added value through their independent activities. Of course, the customer also benefits from the various services and activities these participants offer. Second, in electronic commerce, the number of participants in the platform is more important than who owns it. In general, when the platform creates network effect,[1] it will attract more participants. Third, charging fees for platform use is not a good strategy for attracting participants. Rather, use of the platform should be free of charge or very inexpensive; profits should be generated from indirect sources such as advertisements and sales.

Companies with Offline Platforms

A shopping mall, which situates a variety of independent shops in a certain space, is a type of platform in which suppliers and shoppers are connected. The customer data and information systems of retail companies also play a very significant role for the suppliers in a platform. As an example, Walmart established a strong retail platform by combining its wide logistics network and the associated information systems. As the digital era progressed, Walmart has attempted to establish the stores themselves as platforms.

An Ecosystem of Wide Scope: Walmart

Walmart made a huge investment in its platform in an effort to sustain its rapid growth. It recorded sales of 44.9 billion dollars in 1993; that figure has increased to 5 hundred billion dollars more recently due to the integration of its logistics platform. Since 1993, Walmart has expanded its business platform, creating a business ecosystem including a wide range of supply chain affiliates.

---

[1] The value of a network or platform increases exponentially as more people and more bushinesses become connected. This was explained in the previous chapter.

The Secret of Walmart's Success

Looking into Walmart's business network, we find a success formula other than the well-known one: the everyday low price (EDLP) policy. In short, Walmart's success was possible because of the creation, management, and evolution of a solid business ecosystem. The EDLP policy is rooted on the competitive edge in the Walmart ecosystem. Walmart is accomplishing more than its rivals with the platform strategy, in which the value created from the business is shared with the participants in the ecosystem.

The Walmart ecosystem is a network of many enterprises involved in the distribution process from producers to consumers. Walmart first improved efficiencies in its supply chains. Then, it created a communication route whereby Walmart and its vendors can interact and share information. Finally, the complete Walmart ecosystem was created, fulfilling the company's business strategy thoroughly.

Utilizing its abilities in consumer data collection, Walmart optimizes the production and distribution of thousands of suppliers all over the world. As a result, its ecosystem can provide customers with the products they want when they need them, and at lower prices. Due to these efforts, Walmart outperforms its rivals in terms of cost of goods, profits, and sales per square feet at each store. The Walmart ecosystem has a competitive edge over its rivals for the following reasons. First, trustworthy suppliers are part of the Walmart ecosystem. Secondly, it controls the activities of these suppliers effectively and efficiently. Walmart established its platform to attract excellent suppliers. The advantage to suppliers is that they can gain up-to-date information about customers and fulfill demand with minimal investment or effort. They can obtain this information immediately by connecting their own information systems with the Walmart information system.

The Development of the Walmart Platform: Retail Link®

What are the characteristics of the Walmart platform? The key offering of this platform is customer information. Walmart provides information for the managers of its supply chain. This information is shared with platform affiliates through a variety of interfaces, after which it is processed into a form usable to suppliers. These platforms reduce uncertainty and business complexity for their partners, providing opportunities for innovation.

Walmart's business method has evolved over time, but its ability to obtain up-to-date information has remained constant. Walmart has established the *Retail Link*® system, which provides suppliers with the most up-to-date information in the business world. The Retail Link® is a system that helps the decision-making process, bridging the gap between Walmart and its suppliers. Walmart created, maintains and improves the Retail Link®, helping suppliers make decisions for their mutual benefit based on the information from that link. Any companies supplying products to Walmart can utilize the Retail Link®. From this connection, companies can look up sales data, inventory data, and other Walmart information. They also can place orders through the link.

The efforts of Walmart to build the platform started several decades ago. In 1987, Walmart formed a partnership with P&G to improve efficiency in the supply chain. The Walmart information system was connected with the P&G information system through an EDI(Electronic Data Interchange) link. This move had tremendous effects. It reduced inventory and improved the accuracy of the planning and the inventory management. It also impacted the relationship between these two companies. In short, an antagonistic relationship transformed into a win–win relationship. Since the $6 billion business between P&G and Walmart is so important to both companies, P&G has placed more than 150 employees at Walmart headquarters. Suppliers, such as P&G, are granted the rights to access up-to-date information about how many of its products are being sold at each Walmart store. By contrast, other retail companies protect this information. This is the reason that Walmart suppliers can plan better for production and offer better prices.

Currently, the Walmart Retail Link® acts as a supply chain hub that is connected with the information systems of many manufacturers such as Tyson Foods, Gillette, and P&G. Walmart provides hardware and software that allows its network partners to integrate the Retail Link® with their own supply chains. In addition, through the interface Walmart provides, suppliers can utilize the customer information for value creation in their own companies.

As outlined above, Walmart's platform, which was initially based on customer information, has extended its borders and evolved to include customer networks and merchandising. The information obtained is analyzed and shared with the suppliers through the Retail Link® interface. Building on this information management platform as a foundation, Walmart has created a very efficient distribution system that benefits every member of the business ecosystem.

The Effect of Walmart's Platform

Walmart's goal is to provide a low-cost, high-efficiency platform to support the distribution of a variety of goods. To meet this goal, Walmart provides its suppliers with up-to-date sales data, concentrating on the supply network to achieve economies of scale.

For their part, Walmart's suppliers also made efforts to invest in this platform. This led to system integration between Walmart and its suppliers, a form of CPFR(collaborative, planning, forecasting, and replenishment).[2] Many companies increased productivity, stability, and innovation through CPFR which, in turn, brought Walmart enormous financial gains.

Walmart's Second-Generation Platform

Walmart enjoyed absolute supremacy with its first-generation retail platform. However, recent outcomes have been less stellar than expected due to lack of integration of customers into the business ecosystem. To overcome this weakness, Walmart is developing a second-generation

---

[2] CPFR is an integrated business process through involving collaborative planning, forecasting, and replenishing of goods. Based on the information obtained in this process, both sides benefit due to optimization of production and ordering.

platform combining online and offline sales. Walmart purchased Kosmix in April 2011, building @WalmartLabs with its founders, Venky Harinarayan and Anand Rajaraman. @WalmartLabs is an institute in the Silicon Valley for integration of online and offline platforms.

This second-generation business platform uses the so-called "universal connector", which allows platforms of various businesses to be connected electronically with minimal customization. The key component of this second-generation platform is the analytics platform, which offers answers to various business questions. For example, the analytics platform may answer the questions: What can we sell in our current situation? What are the products customers really want? How can we make profits while facilitating the connection between suppliers and customers?

Walmart is struggling with many problems in this big data era. To resolve its issues, Walmart is establishing the social genome platform (SGP). The SGP analyzes many variables and trends by utilizing outside data such as social media updates, blogs, images, media check-ins, and location information. The analysis results are presented to business affiliates in graph and picture form to help affiliates understand. This information allows Walmart's suppliers and merchandisers to predict the goods in demand effectively and plan accordingly.

The Store is the Platform

Retail companies try to adopt the platform model in an effort to cope with the rapid growth of online distribution companies such as Amazon or eBay. They must transform themselves into platforms by imitating the platform strategies of the online distribution companies. One of these is the "shop-in-shop" concept.

The Birth of the Specialty Department Store: JCPenney

JCPenney has been struggling to escape from a constant sales slump. In 2011, Ron Johnson of Apple was hired as its CEO; Johnson tried to revitalize the company using platform strategy. After adopting the platform strategy of Apple, with particular attention to the case of the

App Store as its reference point, JCPenney moved toward the concept of the "shop-in-shop". By transforming its own department store into a shopping mall, JCPenney tried to be a platform connecting premium brands and shoppers. This was the birth of the first specialty department store.

In a "shop-in-shop", noted brands open their own independent brand shops inside a department store. To extend the comparison with Apple, the brand shop became the equivalent of the app on a smartphone. In addition, the company adopted a new interface. The key to the "shop-in-shop" concept was allowing the operation of premium shops inside the store. Trendy clothing retailers like Joe Fresh, Levi's, and Martha Stewart were recruited. As these brands joined the platform, shoppers began to have new shopping experiences. JCPenney was then able to attract other well-known brands following the success of these premium brands. This, too, increased the potential benefit to shoppers.

Shops doing business in the JCPenney department store were not required to cede their own brand characteristics. After providing a solid platform, JCPenney stepped back from the business dealings of its participants, thus protecting the advantage of having those recruited brands; as a result, JCPenney survived fierce competition.

In addition to the concept of the "shop-in-shop", the street concept also deserves some attention. In its wide corridors, the JCPenney store provided a variety of spectacles and activities, including an iPad island for adults, a LEGO table for children, a coffee bar (Caribou), and a gelato shop (Paciugo Gelato). Shoppers could now stop and have a rest, check their emails, and take care of their children in this wider space. JCPenney tried to upgrade the existing company image through these new store concepts to attract the hip younger generation and change the image of JCPenney as an outdated brand.

Of the 12 JCPenney stores in which the new platform strategy was implemented, a 20% increase in sales was recorded compared to other stores. In the beginning, this new approach seemed to signal the start of a new JCPenney. However, it had its limits; the outcome was less than what was hoped for. Presently, the company is facing a crisis, as Ron Johnson took responsibility and resigned.

Come and Touch It: Best Buy

Like JCPenney, Best Buy also adopted the concept of "shop-in-shop" to overcome low sales and competition from online stores. Best Buy hoped to take advantage of the fame of Samsung, Apple, and Microsoft, taking them as its partners. For their part, Samsung and Microsoft hoped that the loyalty of Best Buy customers would bring success from the partnership. They considered this "shop-in-shop" concept as a tool for expanded product distribution without opening their own stores.

As we observed in the case of JCPenney, the "shop-in-shop" concept is a dangerous one when the retail company lacks a basic competitive edge. Best Buy, however, is solid enough compared to JCPenney. First of all, Best Buy has a stable flow of shoppers who visit the Microsoft, Apple, and Samsung sections at the Best Buy stores.

At JCPenney, the brand and the store have little mutual impact. However, at Best Buy, a synergy effect from the brand and the store can be expected because the Samsung, Microsoft, and Apple brands are far more popular than the brands (Levi's, Liz Claiborne, and Joe Fresh) at JCPenney. In addition, Best Buy is a major retail store, in which all products can be handled. Shoppers can touch, test, and compare these electronic goods at Best Buy stores.

For example, Samsung has opened its Samsung Experience Shops at 1,400 Best Buy stores. Although it is also possible to buy Samsung products at Best Buy, these new shops have Samsung Experience Consultants placed at each location. These consultants provide information about all mobile Samsung products: smartphones, tablets, notebooks, cameras and their accessories. They also help shoppers in testing the products.

While online retailers are taking away customers from traditional retail shops that sell electronics, Best Buy has stationed service experts to sell excellent products of popular brands in its stores. These experts from Samsung, Apple, and Microsoft differ from the existing Best Buy employees. They provide shoppers with interesting and valuable product experiences that they cannot receive from online stores.

The Evolution of Collaboration: Open Innovation

Among the various cases of platform strategy, *open innovation* presents a unique situation. Open innovation means that R&D activities involve the collaboration of many participants on the platform rather than being confined to collaboration within the company.

Innovation by a company usually involves R&D (research and development). The research involves identifying basic technology and development involves commercializing the basic technology to production. Traditionally, R&D has occurred within the company under tight security. The main reason was to keep R&D secret, and the other reason was that it was hard to find external companies with which to collaborate.

For example, take the case of how the smartphone was developed. It was not easy to outsource partial production for things like the main circuit or OS software. The development of any given part requires a full understanding of every other part and the direction of product development. It is not easy to find a development partner with the necessary knowledge and capability. Even when such a company is identified, the costs of communication for collaborative work were so high that it made more sense to develop products in-house.

These days, change is the norm with R&D. More companies utilize basic technology from outside companies through outsourcing. Other companies do things the other way around. More companies produce goods by transferring their basic technology to outside companies. This is called *open innovation*. Open innovation is a process in which anybody is allowed to participate in the R&D process in order to achieve innovation.

Must We Develop for Ourselves?: P&G

P&G is a global producer of food and daily supplies. Several years ago, P&G planned the production of Pringles potato chips, on which puzzles and cartoon figures for advertisement are printed. It was expected to take about two years to develop the product on its own from R&D through to the production process. After searching for individuals or institutes with applicable technologies, P&G found a bakery in Italy with the technology of printing on cakes. The company signed a technology transfer contract with that bakery. P&G began to develop the product as planned utilizing the purchased technology. Through this process, P&G could develop the new product in half the time.

P&G recognized the significance of open innovation and its effects after its success with Pringles. Therefore, it began producing goods through the purchase of outside technology for more than half of its new products, labeling this process C&D (connect and develop), in contrast with R&D (research and development).

Pringles prints from P&G

The Open Innovation Platform of P&G

P&G's Own Platform

P&G developed a platform connecting seventy pioneers in technology and its major suppliers.

* The technology entrepreneurs: P&G's technology entrepreneurs all over the world produce reports on market needs, the influence of related industries on their technologies, and solutions to various technological problems, through their networks with academics and industry researchers.
* Major suppliers: The top 15 suppliers of P&G have 50,000 R&D personnel. To utilize these assets, P&G established an IT platform to share technology reports with its major suppliers. After this, co-development projects with these suppliers increased by 30%.

Outside Platforms

* NineSigma: A platform connecting companies, colleges, government, research institutes, and consultants for the purpose of solving scientific and technological problems.
* InnoCentive: A platform providing solutions to more concrete problems.
* YourEncore: A platform in which over 800 retired scientists and engineers from 150 companies participate for short-term R&D contracts.
* Yet2.com: An online marketplace for the exchange of intellectual property. This platform helps to solve technological problems.

Trade the Technology: InnoCentive

P&G is a case of companies opening R&D to the outside. The next step is for an independent third party to connect companies that are in need of R&D to companies and institutes with expertise in the relevant field. InnoCentive is a good example of this.

InnoCentive is a kind of market where companies in need of technology and product development are the customers, and companies or institutes with the required skills are the suppliers. It is essentially a market for R&D. The customers suggest a price, and the suppliers are compensated accordingly, with the execution of R&D to meet their needs.

Today, a vast amount of R&D is ongoing around the world. Therefore, there is a strong possibility that a company or institute has already developed the technology that is needed by a given company. In the past, there was almost no way to determine who had a needed technology, or who needed an already developed technology. That was why many existing technologies disappeared or were redeveloped over and over again. InnoCentive is a place where technologies can be traded.

InnoCentive is a sort of platform for R&D, since the trades happen systematically and repeatedly at one site. It is also an open platform because all consumers and suppliers of technologies can participate.

Why Open Innovation?

In the past, R&D occurred behind closed doors not only for security reasons, but also due to the difficulties of open collaboration with outside partners. First of all, not many outside agents (individuals or institutes) had technology that was useful to businesses. Moreover, these outside agents were difficult to find even if they had the necessary qualities. When one was found, collaboration was difficult because of the communication problems associated with geographic distance.

For a company to collaborate with another company, to develop a certain product two or three decades ago, it was necessary to identify any available partners and choose the ideal partner for the project. Even if the appropriate company was found and contracts were signed, the work itself would involve overcoming many barriers. Much time and effort would be required in making appointments, holding business meetings, finding meeting places, and sharing information. Moreover, the cost was high in terms of time and financial resources to gain understanding of the work and the organizational

structure of the partner company, which is key for successful collaboration. Therefore, the closed system of R&D was generally much
easier and more efficient.

However, with the development of the Internet and advances in
information technology, these problems have been resolved. First of
all, the Internet brought *information symmetry*, which means that all
individuals and companies have equal access to information and
knowledge. It used to be true that large companies and institutes had
more information and knowledge than small companies or individuals. Today, thanks to the Internet, outside agents, individuals, or
institutes can produce technology on par with or better than that of
anybody else. Moreover, finding and engaging those individuals and
institutes are now much easier.

Once the appropriate collaboration partner is selected, there is no
significant communication problem regardless of location. The
Internet provides a large variety of communication tools like email,
chatting, social networks, video conference calls, bulletin boards, and
online storage services (e.g. Google Drive). It even allows program
sharing through connected computer systems.

In this new environment, open innovation became possible, and
it is now the norm. In short, open innovation is not a newly developed R&D method, but one that arose from the changing
environment.

Platform Strategy for the Latecomer: Xiaomi

One of the companies attracting attention in the smartphone industry
is Xiaomi of China. This company was established in 2010. It is well-
known for selling high-performance Android smartphones at low
prices.

This company is famous for its marketing method, imitating that
of Apple. When the CEO comes out on the stage to introduce the
company's new product, he wears jeans and a black T-shirt, just like
Steve Jobs did. The company develops and produces one product a
year. In addition, loyal young fans of Xiaomi are targeted. These are
some of the ways Xiaomi is imitating Apple. Many people have

considered Xiaomi as nothing more than a weird company, copying everything Apple does.

Xiaomi products
Source: Ilya Plekhanov / CC BY-SA 4.0)

Software as a Competitive Weapon

This impression of Xiaomi has changed since 2014. During that period, the company's market share in China was 14%, surpassing Samsung's 12%. Xiaomi became the 4th largest global smartphone company in 2018.[3] This shows how fast Xiaomi is growing.

This rapid growth of Xiaomi is due to its analysis of the smartphone market as moving from a premium product-oriented one to one oriented toward low-priced products of good quality. While it is easy to think that Xiaomi's competitive edge is based on manufacturing, since it is selling low-priced phones, the company's main competitive edge is in fact, the software.

The CEO of Xiaomi, Lei Jun, is an engineer who knows the potential of software for the smartphone. Xiaomi's first product was

---

[3] http://gs.statcounter.com/vendor-market-share/mobile

not the smartphone, but the software inside the smart phone, MIUI. At present, operating systems used in smartphones range from Google's Android, Apple's iOS to Microsoft's Windows, and so on. The Android operating system is basically an open source software. Companies using the Android system, like Samsung, add their own software to the system, modifying it for use in their phones. For example, the Galaxy Note, which uses the Android system, also includes software from Samsung for its multi-window and pen functions.

On the other hand, the AOSP (Android open source project) is more faithful to the open source spirit of the Android system. Volunteers and certain software developers produce a variety of ROM (read only memory), allowing smartphone users to take advantage of it. To be more precise, ROM is a type of hardware inside smart phones, and some software must be installed on that hardware. Users download the software and install it on their smartphone's ROM. Since AOSP ROM is simpler than the Android on the Samsung smartphone, it is faster and takes up less memory space.

MIUI is a type of AOSP ROM that is popular because of its good performance and compatibility with a variety of hardware. Since its introduction, Xiaomi has sold its own smartphone installed with MIUI: the Mi line smartphone.

Xiaomi produces an updated version of MIUI every other week. Regardless of which Android system-based phone a person is using, the Mi smartphone or others, users can use the upgraded OS without limitations. Since a new version comes out every other week, Xiaomi provides excitement and serendipity to users; this sets it apart from other Android system phones.

Profiting from the Playground

Let us now take a look at how the MIUI software operates as a platform. Every smartphone user needs the OS, since it is the most basic software for the functioning of a smartphone. Samsung uses the Android system. Since Android is provided by Google, Samsung has almost no influence on the core functions of the OS on its phones. On the other hand, Xiaomi has control over the OS on its phones, because most parts of the MIUI are controlled by Xiaomi itself.

Although Google developed and sells Android, the company actually makes profits from ads and transaction fees at its app store, called Google Play. Likewise, Xiaomi has adopted the strategy of providing hardware and software for free or at a very low price in order to expand its share of the market, after which it makes profits based on this foundation. This strategy is similar to that in the game console market.

The company will expand their platform, Mi phones and MIUI software, making profits from the transactions happening there. For this strategy to be successful, it is important to distribute the hardware at the lowest price possible. For this purpose, Xiaomi has simplified its line of devices and minimized marketing costs by advertising only through social network services. Also, it has eliminated the distribution margin through direct online sales.[4] As a result, Xiaomi has developed a device with a similar level of performance to that of Samsung and Apple at about one third of their price. Furthermore, it has also produced a smart TV, tablets, and other IoT (Internet of Things) devices based on expanded versions of MIUI and are priced far cheaper than its rivals.

Xiaomi's Low Price Strategy

The strategy of Xiaomi is very similar to that of Apple's iTunes. The iOS is a platform which comes with the hardware, the iPhone. Apple allows various outside developers to produce apps and contents that operate on the iOS. It makes money by letting these apps and contents be traded on iTunes. Likewise, Xiaomi presents the MIUI, the OS of its smartphone, as a platform where various individuals and companies can do business. Xiaomi then makes profits from this trade.

The difference between Apple and Xiaomi is that Apple charges a high price for its hardware as a premium device. On the other hand, Xiaomi pursues a low price strategy. Since Xiaomi is the latecomer in the

---

[4] TechHolic, 2014/8/18, http://techholic.co.kr/archives/20556

smartphone market, in comparison to Apple, high priority was placed on expansion of its platform. This strategy seems to have worked well so far.

There are mixed views on the future of Xiaomi. Some expect that its success will continue, but others think that Xiaomi will struggle to expand its business outside of China. Since a part of its success has depended on the protectionism of the Chinese government and the patriotism of the Chinese consumers, there may be limits in terms of patent or brand power when Xiaomi products compete in the global market. In any case, Xiaomi is a good example of how a latecomer can successfully utilize platform strategy.

Incheon International Airport: Offering Excitement

Is Incheon International Airport (IIA) a station or a platform? From a purely functional point of view, a station is a place where the bus or train stops. From the perspective of customers, a platform is a space in the business ecosystem where people move around and look for excitement. In that sense, IIA is a platform.

Not a Station, but a Platform

The Incheon International Airport (IIA) made a profit of about $1 billion USD in 2017. In contrast, many international airports focus on providing social infrastructure rather than making profit. For example, the Chicago O'Hare International Airport (ORD) is huge, but fails to make money. On average, passengers spend $6 per person at O'Hare, whereas passengers at IIA spend $49. What is the secret? The answer is that O'Hare is a station, whereas IIA is a platform.

IIA has supremacy over other airports as a business ecosystem with 570 companies and 35,000 workers. Passengers at IIA receive services from these workers as soon as they arrive. First, the immigration control ecosystem leads them into the airport. They usually spend 12 to 16 minutes in the immigration process. This is the fastest immigration service in the world. The time saved is then spent in the shopping ecosystem. Even after shopping, passengers still have extra time to enjoy a fine dining experience. The result is that IIA passengers spend $40 on average shopping and another $9 on food during their time at IIA.

In contrast, at Chicago O'Hare, employees may come across as terse and the service is affected by delays. Passengers must arrive two hours before their flights, but they spend most of this time at immigration and check-in services. If they are lucky, they board the plane after having a hamburger. This is why visitors spend only $6 on average at the O'Hare Airport.

Since IIA is a fun airport with fast service, even the Tsing Tao citizens of China choose Incheon over Shanghai when they go to the U.S., since it takes less time. IIA charges $10 for each transfer passenger. Since 8 million passengers transfer at the Incheon Airport each year, it makes $80 million in profit annually from transfer fees.

As noted above, the success of IIA involves its sub-ecosystems in the areas of immigration, shopping, and transit. This platform strategy allows IIA to claim that it is the world's most fun airport for shopping and transferring.

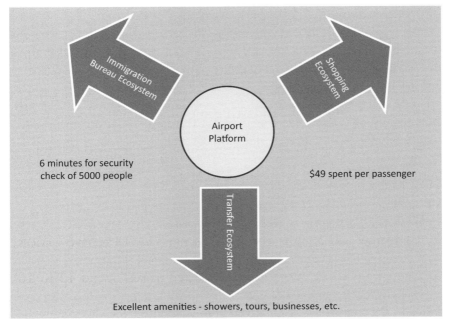

Incheon International Airport as a platform

Success and Failure of Platform Strategy

Platform Evolution of 3M

3M is a company that claims longevity as one of its assets. It was founded in 1902. Its annual sales exceed $32 billion. 3M is one of a few companies that have been included in the Dow Jones Industrial Average for more than 30 years.

3M's secret is that it constantly provides reasons for customers to revisit the company's platform. The firm distributes more than 60,000 kinds of products to 210 countries in the world; it is a platform that provides a set of solutions (PASS1) for our everyday lives. Since it has such a wide variety of products, even its employees do not know about these in entirety.

The 3M ecosystem includes 7 major sub-ecosystems in the areas of film, displays, ceramics, abrasives, nanotechnology, vapor, and orthodontics. These ecosystems entail 46 global technologies. 3M holds so many technologies because it is never complacent with the existing products. It constantly analyzes customer demand and tries to provide solutions to everyday problems.

Forty-six basic, key technologies for production are on the 3M platform. The company accumulates new technology by integrating its existing technologies, constantly innovating. This is the power engine of the 3M platform.

The company's innovations have also been recognized objectively. Business Week ranked 3M third among the 100 most innovative companies in the world after Apple and Google. There is a saying that innovation is like snow fallen yesterday that melts today. Constant innovation is the key to the longevity of 3M.

Provide the Solution, Increase Satisfaction

There are two main strategies for a successful platform, as mentioned above. One is the provision of solutions through killer contents (PASS1 strategy). The other is enhancing the experience of users, thereby increasing their desire to revisit (PASS2 strategy). 3M invests 5 to 6 percent of its sales in R&D to find solutions with killer contents and to improve customer satisfaction. For these purposes, 3M employs scientists and engineers in 85 research centers all over the world.

3M releases several hundred new products every year. Customers purchase those products with no reservations. About 80% of the company's sales come from products developed within the last 4 years. In addition, more than 20% of its sales come from new products. Clearly, 3M has been at the center of change for the last 120 years, ensuring its survival.

The mission of the 3M company is to provide solutions to problems in our everyday lives through constant innovation. The mission statements of 3M are "Improving lives each day" and "To solve unsolved problems innovatively". Peter Drucker, a guru in management, says that the starting point of management is the company mission. Managers should pay constant attention to determine if the company is accomplishing its mission and if employees are keeping the mission in mind.

The management philosophy of 3M can be summarized in the statement, "Never say no to a new product idea". With this philosophy as its foundation, 3M has implemented as its principle of action the "10%, 30%, 15% rule" for the evolution of its platform. The 10% rule states that sales of new products each year must be 10% of the company's total sales. The 30% rule states that 30% of the company's total sales should come from products introduced to the market in the last 5 years. Lastly, the 15% rule states that researchers should be allowed to do whatever they want to do for 15% of their working hours. In many cases, employees spend this free time researching new products and technologies and coming up with their own creative ideas. With its "10%, 30%, 15%" principle, 3M has realized the virtuous cycle of "innovation-new products-sales-R&D".

3M's 15% Principle

The 15% principle was created and completed by William L. McKnight, who was the CEO of 3M from 1949 to 1966. McKnight believed that the creativity of the company depended on its people. Therefore, he tried to create an organizational culture that encouraged employees to share new ideas. The 15% principle arose this way. 3M researchers can work on projects of their own with no interference from management. 3M calls this the "McKnight Principle". It is utilized as part of a creative company culture.

Successful Innovation and Failed Improvement

Some companies succeed in terms of innovation, but fail in terms of sales. Nokia, Kodak, and Motorola are examples of very creative companies with multiple patents and innovative products. However, they failed to make the connection between innovation and sales. Nokia was the first company to develop the smartphone; however, Nokia managers did not focus on the smartphone because they worried it would take over the market of the feature phone, which was the company's major product at the time. Kodak was the first company to develop digital camera technology; however, this innovative technology was ignored while the company continued to focus on the film market. Nokia and Kodak have now disappeared from the business world.

In contrast, 3M is enjoying its longevity. Its platform has evolved with an emphasis on the sales of new products. In 1991, due to economic depression in the United States, 3M was unable to provide its employees with a salary increase for 4 years. Most companies in this situation chose to undergo a restructuring process, but 3M made a different choice.

The CEO at the time, Livio D. DeSimone, chose instead to produce new goods. He actually increased the ratio of new product sales to total sales from 25% to 30%. Until then, 3M had had the 25% principle, which states that the sales of new products should make up 25% of total sales. In the middle of this economic depression,

DeSimone increased that expectation to 30% in order to accelerate innovation in various fields.

DeSimone believed that the company could maintain sustainability as long as innovation remained constant. These innovations resulted in successful sales. However, no matter how magical a new technology is, it is impossible for a company to continue growing with only one technology. As a result, 3M grew until it was holding more than 30 key technologies in the late 1990s.

Recently, the innovation cycle of 3M has shortened such that the 30% principle has evolved into a 40% one. This means that among all the company's sales, 40% must come from products introduced in the last 4 years. As long as 3M constantly strives for innovation, it will not fall into the 'Innovation Paradox', as Kodak and Nokia did.

Failure of Interplay: Pet.com

Pet.com was an online site that sold a variety of pet-related products. It was established in November 1998. Customers could order various kinds of pet products online. Also, they could get premium services, information, and advice from pet experts, including veterinarians.

Pet.com was popular because its prices were sometimes lower than those in the offline market, although the company absorbed the losses. Taking advantage of the dot-com craze, the company sought recognition through hit advertisements and promotions. It seemed to be on the right track when it was listed on the NASDAQ in February 2000. However, it was not able to withstand continuous losses; the company closed its doors in November 2000, only 2 years after its establishment.

Why Pet.com Failed

The failure of Pet.com happened for many reasons. First of all, there was no business strategy unique to Pet.com compared with its rivals. In marketing, it failed in terms of market analysis and targeting. For instance, many customers prefer to buy pet products on their way home or while out shopping. Since online orders require 3 or 4 days for the goods to arrive, customers were naturally reluctant about the service. From the financial point of view, the problem was that the company spent all its investment money before it reached a sustainable economic level. Finally, Pet.com spent too much money on advertisements and in maintaining low prices for the purpose of gaining public recognition.

From the platform perspective, Pet.com failed due to the fact that it pursued the piping business strategy rather than a platform strategy. Pet.com basically assumed the role of a pipe, gathering (sourcing) the pet-related items and selling (transmitting) them to customers. Because the piping business is one-directional, there is no interplay between the participants (suppliers and customers, in the case of Pet.com). To sustain the business, the company had to sell its goods at lower prices than its rivals. In the piping structure, the suppliers had no reason to sell their products to Pet.com at lower prices. Of course, Pet.com must have had a business plan for the time after they secured enough participants. However, based on their actions thus far, the piping strategy seems more evident than the platform strategy.

Pet.com was the first seeable pet-related online business, and initially, business recognition was high. Therefore, it could have evolved as a platform. If Pet.com had attempted a platform strategy and secured a variety of participants, potential customers, and value added suppliers, and if the company had tried to add values through the interplay of participants, it might have enjoyed enormous success.

Platforms in Transitional Periods: Social Commerce

The original meaning of social commerce is a combination of social relations and shopping. For example, social network services, such as Facebook and Instagram, allow people to share information about the costs of goods with their friends or acquaintances when they are considering going shopping. These activities on social networks involving shopping are called "social commerce". In a sense, TicketMonster, Coupang, and WeMakePrice[5] in Korea are

---

[5] Groupon in the U.S. was a similar company.

considered under the group purchase category rather than under the social commerce umbrella. The main purpose of these businesses is to offer goods at low prices through the group purchasing option; the interplay among people is not part of the process. At any rate, we will call it "social commerce" in this analysis.

The Profit Structure of Social Commerce

Social commerce is growing so fast in Korea that its sales are expected to reach $17 billion USD in 2018. We now examine how social commerce is understood from the platform point of view.

The business structure of social commerce is as follows. First, a seller applies to sell goods/services at a social commerce company at lower prices in the hope of high-volume sales at a low unit margin of profit. Alternatively, a social commerce company finds a seller who wants to sell its goods/services at lower prices. These goods/services are listed in the social commerce company's website as a 'deal'. Then, buyers purchase the goods/services.

Delivery is usually the seller's responsibility. When the seller receives notice from the social commerce company about the order, the seller delivers the goods directly to the consumer. Some social commerce companies have their own delivery networks and can be in charge of delivery. Also, for goods and services that require a store visit, like restaurants, sales coupons are sent to customers in print or electronically.

Most social commerce companies profit from the 15 to 20 percent fees over and above the sales price. In addition, the sale of 'undeemed' coupons is another source of revenue for social commerce companies. From the seller's perspective, advertisements informing people about their products is the main benefit. Businesses with low variable costs such as esthetic services enjoy the benefits of higher turn-over rates. Of course, sellers must pay some costs since they provide goods and services at discounted prices; however, they often consider this loss as part of their advertisement costs.

Social Commerce from the Platform Perspective

From the platform perspective, social commerce has the potential to evolve into a platform, but it may take some time before it can properly be called a platform. As a platform, the primary role of the social commerce company is to connect sellers to buyers. As sellers try to increase awareness of their brands, their goods are sold at low prices to buyers who are searching for goods at cheap prices. At this point in business history, social commerce only plays this minor role. Therefore, from the seller's standpoint, there is no reason to use social commerce if similar benefits can be realized from the effects of advertisement at a similar cost. From the buyer's standpoint, if a lower price is offered elsewhere, there is no reason to purchase goods through the social commerce company.

In short, social commerce is currently a simple connecting link between sellers and buyers. Therefore, trade between these parties is often a one-shot deal. At present, social commerce does not have the characteristics of a platform, in which new value is created through the interplay of platform participants. From the solution or multi-sided market point of view, any connection between the seller and buyer that is based only on price and ends as a one-shot trade is considered a transaction that takes place through the solution approach. It has yet to create an ecosystem in which added value is offered.

Social commerce involves a simple equation between the price and the group of buyers; it involves the search for sellers who are willing to offer the goods at lower prices. On the other hand, it involves spending a lot of money on advertisement and marketing to attract more buyers. As a result, social commerce companies in contemporary Korea continually report losses. In 2018, the top 3 social commerce companies in Korea reported a cumulated loss of $2.5 billion USD.

Of course, fierce competition that makes companies willing to take losses will occur due to the salient characteristic of this scenario: that there is only one survivor in the end. However, even if a company succeeds and becomes the sole survivor in its field, it is difficult to guarantee its survival based on this simple value structure because once online shopping malls and home shopping, as well as social network services such as Facebook or WhatsApp, join the social network-based commerce business world, the competition with these companies must be very difficult to handle.

Part II

Platform as a Successful Business Strategy

Chapter 05

Characteristics of Successful
Platform Strategy

- Why Platform Strategy?
- Platform over Device
- Ecosystem Structures
- Formula for a Successful Platform
- Golden Rules for Platforms

Earlier, we examined companies that succeeded, failed, or are in transition. As these examples demonstrate, adoption of the platform strategy does not always lead to success. In order to succeed, we must understand the characteristics of a successful strategy and how to apply it. Let us now examine the characteristics of a successful platform strategy.

Why Platform Strategy?

Modularization and the Rise of Platform Business

In manufacturing, platform strategy is related to modularization, which is a way to produce a variety of products by combining many interchangeable parts, like LEGO blocks. For example, let us say that a product consists of three parts: A, B, and C. Let us assume that A has 5 variations, B has 3, and C has 4. Depending on how these parts and variations are combined, 60 different models can be produced ($5 \times 3 \times 4 = 60$).

Modularization provides the advantage that it can satisfy a variety of consumer needs. Global companies can also utilize this strategy to localize their products. In fact, adopting the platform approach in manufacturing means simplification via modularization. Producing a variety of goods with the same key module (platform) by adding different submodules is essentially the platform-based manufacturing approach.

The modular (platform) approach makes a difference only in terms of production efficiency in cases where all the parts necessary are produced within the company. However, it is a different story if some parts for the products come from outside the company. The producer of the key module is an especially important player. In fact, as the modular process gained popularity, the trend was that the controller of the key module (the platform) enjoyed supremacy in the market. From the late 20th century, the modular system has improved so rapidly that many platform companies have arisen.

Closed, Converged Devices: The Case of IBM

From the 1970s to the early 1980s, the structure of the computer industry was very vertical. Large companies, including the three largest, IBM, DEC, and HP, had very integrated business structures. They purchased many subparts from third parties but produced and supplied their own operating systems, application software, hardware, and even peripheral devices.

At the time, products and systems in the computer industry had integrated architecture. In other words, the system of one company's computer was not interchangeable with that of another company's computer. For example, DEC software could not be operated on an IBM computer, and the other way around. Therefore, each company developed proprietary technology necessary for the production of almost all the subparts necessary to run their systems.

IBM, during this period, had absolute power in the market, and made a lot of money. By sustaining the closed and integrated architecture of IBM computers, the company retained its existing customers for a long time. IBM blocked competition from its rivals, who had strengths only in one area of hardware, software, or service, by emphasizing the value of the IBM systems and service package.

From Vertical to Horizontal Structure

From the late 1970s, IBM faced a new challenge. Out of the blue, Apple computers came out. Apple produced a product called the "personal computer", which was worthless according to IBM. However, the personal computer gained popularity among "expert" customers, who were increasing in number in the electronics and computer market.

In response, IBM established a new operation division, in which it produced its own personal computers. However, the new PC division did not take the vertically integrated architecture approach. Instead, IBM adopted a modular architecture approach, purchasing the microprocessor from Intel and the operating system from Microsoft. These were then assembled to form a computer, the IBM PC.

The computer that took over the market after that was an IBM PC clone, not the IBM PC. IBM's modular approach allowed large and small companies to join the platform, supplying subparts such as semiconductor chips, mainboards, applied software, peripheral devices, network services, PC design tools, and assembly tools. As a result of the decision-making of one major producer, IBM, to make the change from a vertically integrated industry structure to a horizontal modular structure, significant structural change occurred in the whole market. This structural change brought a huge change to the industry as a whole. As the PC subparts made by Intel and Microsoft became available to everyone, many businesses appeared in the IBM PC clone computer market.

The Birth of Platform Strategy

As we learned from the development of the PC and changes in the computer industry, industrial structures that are vertical and integral are pressured to become modular once a certain level of business activity is reached. There are usually three situations in which dismantling is necessary in an existing vertical and integral industry structure: (1) as in the case of the PC, when many competitors enter a niche market; (2) when the integral structure is losing its efficiency because of the complexity of the system; (3) when companies within an industry have a serious bureaucracy problem and their organizational structures become inflexible.

Once modularization was under way in the PC industry, PC assembly companies like Samsung, Compaq, and Dell jumped in. In addition, companies like Intel and Microsoft began gaining power. As time went by, the companies that gained market control were those supplying key modules like the microprocessor or OS, not the assembly companies. Therefore, Intel and Microsoft became the key power players in the industry. Moreover, these two companies added their own new functions to the key modules (platforms) that they provided. At the same time, they began to support complementary developers that produced and sold goods based on their modules. This was the birth of platform strategy in the computer market.

The Evolution of Apple through Open Platform Strategy

In the 1980s, even though IBM PC clones dominated the market, no singular company dominated the platform. Rather, the suppliers to manufacturers of IBM PC clones, such as Microsoft and Intel, became dominant on the platform. Because IBM adopted an open modular strategy to compete with Apple, Apple can be considered a contributor to the modular development of the PC industry. However, Apple itself turned to an integrative strategy rather than a modular one in order to sustain the benefits of its monopoly. IBM's modular strategy created fierce competition in the PC market, which paved the way for Microsoft and Intel to become the platform leaders.

In the 1980s, Apple's Macintosh computer was an excellent product with far more advanced technologies than that in other PC companies. However, Apple did not recognize that the unique quality of its Macintosh computer lay not in its software and hardware package, but in the operating system (platform). As a result, Apple made the mistake of binding a superior operating system with inferior hardware. Meanwhile, the IBM PC clones surpassed Apple in the market through fierce competition in subsystems among themselves.

However, Apple succeeded several decades later with the iPod and iPhone because it chose a vertical open platform strategy. Although its closed strategy regarding its hardware and operating system remains in place, Apple's App store is an excellent example of an open strategy.

Success with Support from the Market

From the market's point of view, a platform leader controls the market because the platform and its complementors offer outstanding efficiency and serendipity. For instance, Microsoft Windows comes with various types of software based on this system, and the Android or iOS allows users to enjoy various, high-quality mobile apps. Although a platform may be outstanding, if it is not supported by the market, it cannot be successful. If the Android platform is to succeed, there should be many app developers, telecom companies, and smartphone manufacturers who adopt the Android system. In addition, many consumers must be willing to use the machines or services based on this operating system.

The "Intel Inside" campaign was an effort to obtain strong platform status by connecting two major Intel customers: the computer manufacturer and the computer buyer. Intel cooperated strategically with Microsoft with its "Wintel" (Windows and Intel) campaign also for this purpose.

Platform over Device

Paradigm for Interplay

The traditional business model focused on management in a one-sided market with a value flow of "produce → sell". In a one-sided market, the key is in the development of the device (hardware product) and efficiency in management. A company competes with its rivals through superior production of better goods and higher sales based on management innovation.

However, it is now impossible for one company to satisfy all the needs of its customers. Presently, to develop a smartphone or hybrid car requires 7,000 and 60,000 patents respectively. In the past, one product was associated with one patent. Today, even manufacturing a golf ball involves about 50 patents. Therefore, the paradigm under which a company operates depends on the market in which it is located. The consumer paradigm focused on the one-shot trade is giving way to a paradigm that emphasizes the interplay among participants within the ecosystem.

Ecosystem Wars

In the consumer paradigm focusing on the one-shot trade, the company that provides better products or services has a competitive edge in the market. However, today's products and companies are more complex than in the past. Computer hardware and software is used in the everyday lives of most consumers. As these products increase in complexity, it becomes more difficult for a single company to remain competitive alone. For business success, the cooperation of many related companies is required.

Automobile, smartphone, and game companies must have constant interaction with many related companies and organizations. They must also manage the ecosystem and their customers at the same time. The days are gone when a consumer simply buys a device and consumes it. Consumers of today utilize a multitude of products in their everyday lives and enjoy the use of various contents; in this process, they pay more attention to the experience of the interplay among products, components, and companies.

As society becomes more specialized, the roles of intermediaries, such as credit card or real estate agents, gain significance and platform businesses gain importance. An example is that of Facebook, which was developed by Mark Zuckerberg at Harvard. In using the platform business model, Facebook has now become a company with enormous market value. For business success, the battle of devices must end, and the war of ecosystems must begin. Individual companies must avoid micro-management strategies focusing on profits through product sales. Strategic efforts must be made to plan and evolve ecosystems, or economic spaces for the interplay of participants; in other words, the platform is the new key to success.

Platform Leadership

Companies based on traditional business models can also find opportunities by transforming themselves into platforms. Establishing a new platform can provide competitive advantages in the traditional market. Both two-sided and multi-sided market platforms are currently being developed.

A multi-sided market platform requires many interrelated participants who create a business ecosystem together. In order to create a business ecosystem, it is necessary to make the value proposition attractive to potential participants. This is the role of platform leaders, or "platformers". Platformers plan and manage the platform. They are responsible for building community, providing space, minimizing costs, controlling the payment function, and so on. In addition, they must plan an attractive platform space that provides excitement and serendipity in addition to fulfilling the platform's basic functions. The benefits that ecosystem members enjoy from participating in the platform will induce them to stay for a long time. Through the efforts of the platformer, as the platform evolves, participants' satisfaction will increase, and business outcomes will improve.

In the Same Boat

In visualizing the evolution of the platform, rather than thinking of picking individual fruits, we should think of harvesting after seeding and nurturing. In a platform situation, the obsession with immediate profit for its own sake makes it difficult to establish consistent, profitable, long-term relationships. Therefore, overcoming the desire for competition with ecosystem members in favor of cooperation is key. Moreover, to expand the market, active cooperation with rivals is also necessary.

Platform management is like a voyage in a boat with members who have different interests. In ancient China, a legend was told of people from two hostile countries, Wei and Yue, who got on the same boat. Although their countries were at war, they cooperated with each other when faced with a storm, for they shared the common goal of survival. This legend illustrates that sometimes cooperation with rivals is necessary to maintain the survival of the platform. This principle is important for platform management.

Ecosystem Structures

Ecosystem wars start with a market, whether two-sided or multi-sided, that is transformed into a platform. The platform is where the demand for and supply of the key contents come together. Through cooperation, the members of the ecosystem can enlarge their ecosystem through their business efforts on the platform. The ecosystem grows through the efforts of the complementors and evangelists, after which competition between the ecosystems starts. The structure of this market transition may vary in several ways.

First, in a one-sided market with limited seller–buyer relations, only the buyers are the customers; the sellers have only their own customer ecosystems to manage. In this case, customer satisfaction is the best goal of the business model, and the direction of business is one-way.

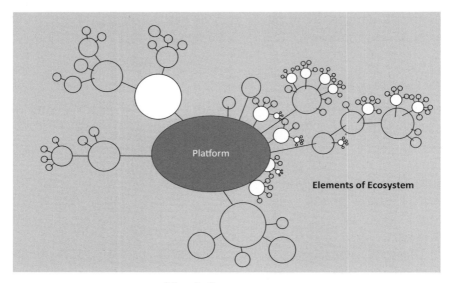

The platform ecosystem

Secondly, in a two-sided market such as credit card, the chain of business relations is "seller–card company–buyer". Here, the card company provides the platform, creating a two-sided market in which transaction fees are collected from the sellers and membership fees from the buyers. In a two-sided market platform, the seller and the buyer are both customers.

In a two-sided market, interplay between sellers and buyers is possible on a single or multiple platforms. Because all parties share the associated costs, they have incentive to trade on the platform. In our example, the card company, which is the platformer, must manage the seller ecosystem and the buyer ecosystem at the same time.

In a two-sided market platform, as the number of participants on one side increases, business opportunities for participants on the other side also increase. This is the virtuous cycle, which is related to positive network externalities. For example, in the relation chain of bees–orchard–flowers, the orchard is the platform in a two-sided market. If there are bee hives in the orchard, the fruit harvest will be better, and positive externalities result for the beekeeping business.

Therefore, the platformer must make space through serendipity and evolution in order to increase the number of revisits. Each platform must have a portfolio that includes many free items and few expensive key products, all of which must be managed.

As a multi-sided market example, the Harvard Business School created a platform including professor–student–company relations. The first component is the professor ecosystem, which attracts the best professors possible by providing them with an attractive workspace. Because there are excellent professors at Harvard, talented students from all over the world come to the school. With this vitalized ecosystem of students, Harvard gains income in the form of tuition. This is not the end of the financial process, however. Harvard also established a development fund based on a supporter ecosystem made up of companies that want the cooperation of excellent professors and their students.

Therefore, Harvard Business School, through the strategy of planning and managing a platform that includes professors, students, and supporters (companies), benefits from the activities of three ecosystems: those of the professors (research funds), students (tuition), and supporters (donations).

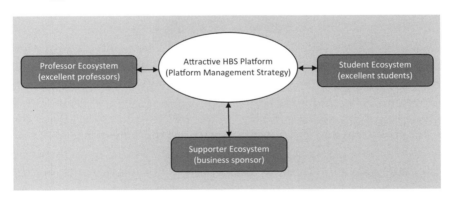

The multi-sided market platform of Harvard Business School

Platform strategy should start with platform management, which involves developing the supplier ecosystem, rather than satisfying the customer through sales of goods. As the platform becomes more attractive, outcomes resulting from platform management will increase.

Formula for a Successful Platform

A platform can be seen as a playground for customers and a container for killer contents. It is both a virtual and a real space where people can gather; through many opportunities for interplay in that space, they eventually form a group.

This interplay for relation building is the starting point of the ecosystem. Rather than making profits from sales, the focus is on retaining customers. Business outcomes depend on strategies of cooperation rather than of competition to win the most sales.

To establish a successful platform, the reason to use the platform should be clear: the killer contents or solutions (PASS1), which are the invisible engine of the platform. For example, for the iPod, music is its killer contents. In addition, for the platform to evolve, there should be a reason for participants to continue to engage in the interplay on the platform: that is, excitement and fun, in other words, serendipity (PASS2). For example, the iPhone is successful, because its complementors keep providing customers with serendipity. For the success of the platform, platform leadership is also necessary in order to support ecosystem partners and keep them producing complementary goods. In short, the formula for platform success is the solution plus serendipity, as shown in the following diagram.

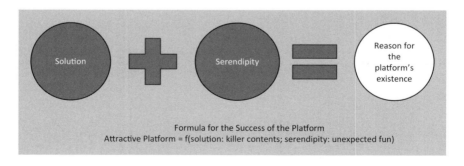

Formula for the Success of the Platform
Attractive Platform = f(solution: killer contents; serendipity: unexpected fun)

The solution (or killer contents) has the power to induce a visit. The platformer alone cannot offer a competitive solution. The power of solution increases as the complementary goods provided by the complementors become richer.

Serendipity has the power to make participants revisit or stay. Therefore, platforms should provide interesting experiences and opportunities for fun in order to be successful. As further good solutions are offered and serendipity grows, the possibility for ecosystem success increases.

Golden Rules for Platforms

There is a classic movie entitled, "The Ten Commandments". The movie is considered a masterpiece; it propelled its leading actor, Charlton Heston, into a Hollywood star. "The Ten Commandments" is based on a story in the Book of Exodus. In the story, God helped the suffering Jews escape Egypt. He gave them the Ten Commandments to prevent them from going back to their depraved lives and old customs.

For a company going through a transitional period, the platform may occupy the role of savior, like Moses who parted the Red Sea and led the Jews to freedom. However, there is no guarantee of success with the platform alone. Success comes only when the conditions for a successful platform are satisfied, and the roles within the platform are well executed. We now outline ten principles for platform success based on the successful platform strategies discussed so far.

1. *The Playground Principle*

A good platform is a well-equipped playground where various stakeholders can cooperate, and interplay can take place. In a desirable playground, platform members and the owner of the playground can all prosper.

The platformer who is managing the playground should not dominate it. Even in the process of expanding the platform, the platformer should be a supporter with the aim of minimum intervention to maintain product/service quality. Too much control over platform participants can harm the platform itself.

Evaluation of platform participants should be done by platform users (the market) with support from the platformer. Also, participant autonomy should be respected, and control over each participant's turf should be kept at a minimum. In short, a good platform is run through a solid facilitator rather than a president.

2. *The Rule of Externality*

Network externality, or "the network effect", means that active trade among parties brings in new customers or new technologies, which in turn create new values and revitalize the platform. The platform leader is responsible for increasing network externality.

When there are many platform users, the platform provides them with opportunities to meet more people. Therefore, their value increases exponentially (direct positive externality). Moreover, as the number of users increases, the complementary goods and applications based on this number would also increase, ultimately increasing the value of the platform (indirect positive externality).

3. *Conductor, not Controller*

The platform leader (platformer) is a value creator and a distributor who considers the interests of every member of the ecosystem. As a conductor, not a controller, the platform leader ensures that companies can coexist in the ecosystem. For sustainability of the platform, the platform leader should not seek to control or steal the benefits of externality. The role of the platform leader is thus very complex.

First of all, the platform leader must mediate and simplify the complex connections among companies on the platform. Second, the platformer should encourage constant technological innovation, guiding and supporting platform participants in adjusting to new and uncertain environments. As the platformer shares information about the future evolution direction of the platform with the developers, the developers should feel comfortable participating in the innovation on the platform. Third, the platformer should provide innovative technology to participants in order to create niches. Niche creation is a phenomenon in which the ecosystem expands with the creation of new business fields based on platform innovation. Finally, the platformer must share the created value with the whole ecosystem. If the platformer monopolizes the created value, participating complementors cannot survive. It is the responsibility of the platformer to consider the survival and prosperity of all participants when harvesting profits from the platform.

4. *The Rule of Honey Bees*

The power of the platform increases as more business partners join the platform, akin to the process of pollination. As honey bees extract nectar from flowers, some pollen sticks to their legs. As the bees move onto the next flower, pollination of the plant can occur, which eventually leads to new fruits and new flowers. This evolution produces the next generation of the ecosystem.

Most platform leaders cannot produce complementary goods for the entire ecosystem alone. Therefore, the power of the platform must be expanded through collaboration with complementors. When the platformer and the complementors work together, the benefits increase for all members of the ecosystem.

5. *The Principle of Openness*

Closed systems that seek answers within themselves lack sustainability, whereas with the open platform system, positive externalities are constantly improving. However, unlike a botanical ecosystem, a business platform is not a completely open garden. Value creation by outside participants is important, but quality management is also important. When product quality is uncontrolled, low-quality and illegal contents may take over the platform. It is like an open garden in which bees and butterflies are free to come and contribute to the ecosystem, but the garden remains vulnerable to attack from worms and wild animals.

Therefore, for platform sustainability, tools to control product quality are necessary, as long as they do not hinder openness. In other words, a platform should have "bounded openness", like a garden with low fences. The desirable level of openness and of control is dependent on the situation.

6. *The Rule of Killer Contents*

Having a platform does not necessarily mean having many participants and users. In order to attract more users to the platform, there should be more existing participants and more quality contents being added. As more users join the platform, there will be more quality contents added, and this will attract more users. To create this virtuous cycle, killer contents must first be offered in order to attract participants and users. In the case of iTunes, music was the killer contents. In the case of Facebook, it was easy communication with acquaintances, and in the case of Amazon, it was products priced cheaper than offline. These killer contents contributed to the growth of the platforms of these companies in their early years.

The killer contents are the key element of platform growth, especially in the early stages, and a good platform always has good, killer contents. However, killer contents are not always goods or services. Killer contents can be anything superior among the so-called "QCDRT" (quality, cost, delivery, reliability, technology).

In the area of social commerce, which was explained in the earlier chapter, the price takes on the role of killer contents. Customers choose their services in spite of the problem of having fewer options and other inconveniences due to low prices. When the number of users increase, more sellers will decide to join the ecosystem, thus leading to the creation of a virtuous cycle. In the beginning stages of a platform, these killer contents attract users and participants. Later, when the platform reaches a certain size, many new services can be offered, or business models can be attempted.

7. *The Principle of Community and Communication*

If the stand-alone piping model is a divisive and rational approach, the platform model is an integral and spiritual approach. In this approach, communication among members of the ecosystem and internal customers is important. In the communication process, long-term blueprints about the future direction of the platform and its evolution should be provided to all participants to encourage systematic innovation and to ensure stability of the ecosystem. In addition, the platformer must build empathy with all partners and be available to resolve potential conflicts of interest. Constant communication is therefore required. An appropriate internal structure can help the platformer manage external and internal conflicts of interest.

In business ecosystems with partners from various industries, there is a strong possibility of conflicts arising. To prevent these conflicts among ecosystem members, a diversity of connections is necessary. When relationships are strong, and interplay occurs among many partners at the same time, conflicts are more easily resolved. Having highly diverse connections results in a wide range of relationships, facilitating broader and deeper interplay between platform participants. Diversity of connections increases understanding of the capability and the characteristics of others, bringing stability to the network.

8. *Boundary Rules*

As time passes, the platform boundaries need to expand. When complementary goods and applications gain popularity, the platform absorbs them and becomes an even bigger platform. The platformer facilitates this absorption of technology and works toward improving its efficiency and stimulating innovation to create new technology and applications. However, if the platformer gets greedy and tries to dominate the new technology or applications, conflicts with complementors/producers may arise. Complementors will resist, perceiving this action on the platformer's part as a prevention or a violation of the creativity of each member of the business ecosystem. In the past, for example, Intel and Microsoft faced resistance from their complementors/producers when they tried to put too many new functions on their microprocessor and Windows systems.

Therefore, to avoid conflicts over borders, the following tenets should be remembered: 1. Share the interface technology while protecting the key technology; 2. Sacrifice short-term interests for the common interests of the industry and the ecosystem; 3. Do not invade the partner's turf; and 4. Support the complementors/producers in protecting their own intellectual property rights.

9. *The Rule of the Intermediary*

The platformer should mediate communications between the various members of the ecosystem, respecting their various interests. The competitive edge of the platform and ecosystem can be sustained through efficient value creation and product distribution. Therefore, the platformer must be the mediator who negotiates the interplay and resolves conflicts among ecosystem members, while also prioritizing its own relations with each member. In this case, the role expected from the platformer is as follows.

First, the platformer is the protector of security. Situations may arise wherein one party fulfils a promise while the other party withdraws from promised payment. To resolve these situations, the platformer must take a significant security from both sides and ensure the execution of the promise. Examples include escrow services, in which Apple or Amazon guarantee the sellers payment. Escrow services are used in general trade and in business transactions, as well as online.

Second, the platformer must act as a deposit preventing information leakage. When two parties try to become partners, they tend not to invest their money unless they have developed enough trust in the capability and the intent of the other party. However, if a company opens its books to provide information in order to gain the other's trust, it may lose negotiation power. Therefore, if a third party obtains information about both sides and provides them only with the necessary information, the problem will be resolved. A good example of this is the seller evaluation system of Amazon. Another example is a technology deposit system, which protects against technology leakage of small companies when they make business deals with large companies.

Third, the platformer acts as mediator for trust building. It should play as an agent when trustworthy partners start a new relationship.

10. *The Rule of Serendipity*

The platform must have fun. A good platform has constant changes, and provides its customers with serendipity and unexpected value that makes customers want to revisit and consume more. The positive experience of the users, called experience economy, results in the growth of the platform.

The secret of a successful platform strategy lies in serendipity. Therefore, to be successful, platforms should evolve from the "platform as a set of solutions (PASS1)" model to the "platform as a serendipitous strategy (PASS2)" model.

	The golden rules of platform	
1	The Playground Principle	A good platform should be a playground where various participants collaborate and enjoy themselves. In a good playground, businesses of not only the members, but also the owner can prosper.
2	The Rule of Externality	Externality means that active trade among parties brings in new customers or new technologies, which in turn creates more value. Platform leaders should strive to increase network externality.
3	Conductor, not Controller	Platform leaders should be conductors, not dominating controllers, of the coexisting platform members. This approach requires not only adequate technology, but also a philosophy of coexistence.
4	The Rule of Honey Bees	As more business partners join, the platform becomes more powerful in the market, similar to the way bees and flowers cooperate to produce the next generation of ecosystem members and contribute to the evolution of the system as a whole.
5	The Principle of Openness	In a closed system, answers are sought inside the company, and sustainability is uncertain. Only the open platform system increases the externality effects and leads to growth.
6	The Rule of Killer Contents	The killer contents are the key to platform growth, and a good platform always has killer contents, which are not necessarily only goods or services. Killer contents can

(Continued)

(Continued)

		be anything superior among the so-called "QCDRT" (quality, cost, delivery, reliability, technology).
7	The Principle of Community and Communication	If the stand-alone piping model is the divisive and rational approach, the platform model is an integral and spiritual approach. For this approach, communication among members of the ecosystem and internal customers is important. In the process of communication, the long-term blueprints for the future direction of the platform and its evolution should be provided to all participants to encourage systematic innovation and to ensure stability of the ecosystem.
8	Boundary Rules	The platform leader should not invade the domains of its partners. If this happens, they will resist, considering this action on the leader's part as a violation of the creativity of each member of the business ecosystem.
9	The Rule of the Intermediary	The platform leader must focus on building relations among the platform members, acting as a mediator who negotiates the interplay and resolves conflicts among the ecosystem members, while also establishing its own relations with each member.
10	The Rule of Serendipity	The platform should be fun. Serendipity or unexpected pleasure is the key to make users revisit the platform and the platform successful.

Chapter 06

Platform Strategy for Success

- Let Them Come and Stay
- Be a Conductor, not a Dominator
- Understand the Nature of the Business
- Platform Architecture Design
- Manage Platform Boundaries
- Develop Platform Strategy

There are many things to consider in establishing
a platform strategy. Those introduced here are things
that should not be neglected in the process of planning
a platform strategy, because doing so will increase the
possibility of failure even after considerable efforts are
made to develop the strategy. Let us not make the mistake
of losing the war with a faulty strategy.

Let Them Come and Stay

Platform Formation and Maintenance

How can we vitalize a platform and encourage its evolution? The answer is simple. Let them come and stay. First, provide the conditions for the platform's establishment. Then, provide the conditions for sustainability. These conditions are essential to the success of platform strategy.

To make a platform desirable for participants to come and stay, it should be a place of expectation and excitement. A platform like Seoul Station is becoming an exciting place for saying farewell, meeting friends, traveling, having breakfast, and shopping. In this example, the train is nothing but the key device. These days, Seoul Station is not just a place to buy train tickets, but a place of excitement. As a result, the station is evolving day by day.

A good platform strategy brings in quality participants and offers its customers excitement. However, there must be some rules on how and who can participate. Efforts must be made to prevent greedy and self-righteous behavior, and consequences for these behaviors are necessary. Through these efforts, the quality and quantity of members in the ecosystem can be maintained at an optimum level. As a result, the level of satisfaction of members of the ecosystem will grow. This is the evolution of the ecosystem. At the beginning stages of the platform, potential members of the business ecosystem should be offered a trial platform visit. Efforts should be made to encourage these participants to stay or repeat the visit.

Strategies for Promoting Revisiting

The platform strategy of "come and stay" can be categorized into the initial trial strategy and the promoting strategy, as discussed below.

Initial Trial Strategy

To encourage the initial visit, the platform concept should be good enough to raise the visitor's expectations. Attractive killer contents are necessary. This is the first stage of platform strategy (platform as a set of solutions, PASS1). In this first stage, the killer contents are the most critical aspect of the platform. The better the killer contents of a platform, the more visitors would visit the platform.

Promoting Strategy

Promoting revisiting entails strategies to make first-time visitors come back. To increase the intention to revisit, a satisfying experience should be provided, which will result in lasting relations. For this to happen, visitors must experience serendipity in their time visiting the platform (platform as a serendipitous strategy, PASS2). The platform should be a place of constant change and evolution, open innovation, and co-evolution within the business ecosystem. As members of the platform evolve, the competitive edge of the platform's business ecosystem should improve.

Why Las Vegas is More Popular than the Great Wall of China

A television program such as "I Am a Singer" or "K-pop Star" is a successful platform model with open innovation. In "I Am a Singer", six competent singers come out and sing an arranged piece of somebody else's music. An evaluation panel of 500 ordinary people judges these singers, eliminating one singer every week. The place of the eliminated singer is occupied by a new singer every week. This program is a contest among many accomplished singers as to who is the best. It is a lively program offering members of the broadcasting ecosystem entertainment.

The "K-pop Star" model operates under the assumption that anybody can be a singer, bringing people from all over the world to the competition. The attraction of hearing many talented artists from all over the world brought viewers to this TV program. The producers of these television programs are the conductors or the facilitators of the program. They allow members of the ecosystem to play in the meadow rather than in a fenced zoo. As a result, millions of viewers found serendipity and enjoyed what the platform had to offer.

The Great Wall of China, which is a world cultural heritage site, has 10 million visitors a year, but Las Vegas, the city of gambling, has 40 million visitors. The Great Wall does not change, so it is enough to visit only once. However, Las Vegas offers different things every time you visit, which is why people keep coming back. Therefore, to increase the number of visitors, a serendipity strategy is important.

It cannot be emphasized enough that a platform without fun is doomed to fail. If serendipity in the platform experience is high, visitors' intent to revisit increases. Therefore, the evolution of the platform depends on the functional balance between the killer contents (solution) and excitement (serendipity). The evolutionary direction of the platform can be understood through the following diagram.

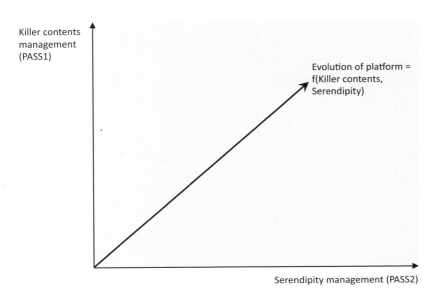

The evolutionary direction of the platform

Be a Conductor, not a Dominator

Sharing or Plundering

America Online (AOL) and Yahoo enjoyed their heyday in the internet business field at the end of the 20th Century. They wielded strong power in the world of internet commerce based on their large customer base. As shown in the following diagram, America Online and Yahoo took the traditional approach in their business deals with partner companies.

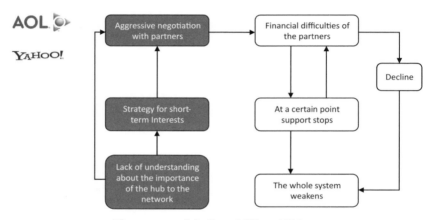

The process of decline: AOL and Yahoo

America Online and Yahoo obtained so many members during the internet boom. In the world of the internet, many members equals high property value (customer assets). Therefore, America Online and Yahoo, with their large customer assets, were in a position to make advantageous negotiations with other internet companies. These two companies utilized their negotiating power to obtain maximum profits in deals with other internet companies such as content providers. In fact, they demanded the maximum fees their internet partners could afford.

However, this approach made it difficult for the partner companies to profit. As many partners found it difficult to survive, the ecosystems centering on AOL and Yahoo became less attractive. As a result, AOL and Yahoo faced a crisis. Yahoo restructured its internet strategy with a long-term perspective, which allowed the company to be revived. On the other hand, AOL, which was the world's largest internet company at the time, met its demise.

Virtuous or vicious cycles can also be found in the histories of eBay and Enron. eBay and Enron are similar in that they prospered with the development of IT. However, their fate varied according to their views of the business ecosystem. Enron saw the business ecosystem as an opportunity to plunder; that company disappeared, while eBay saw the business ecosystem as a matter of coexistence, and that company survived.

Enron tried to create maximum value. As in the cases of AOL and Yahoo, it negotiated numerous concessions from its partners. On the other hand, eBay shared the value created with its partners. Rather than pursuing short-term profit, eBay tried to establish an ecosystem that included a wide range of healthy trade partners with a long-term perspective.

Conductor Strategy vs. Dominator Strategy

The successful case of eBay shows the effectiveness of a desirable, profit-sharing approach between a platform leader and partner companies; the relationship between this approach and the direction of the business ecosystem is obvious. The traditional dominator's strategy involves one company taking most of the profits by using its position in the business ecosystem to advantage. By contrast, eBay pursued a virtuous cycle strategy of improving the health of the ecosystem as a whole to create more value. Through this virtuous cycle, the platformer can continue to expect good outcomes. This "conductor" strategy of contributing to the virtuous cycle of the whole ecosystem is very different from trying to gain profits by controlling or dominating business activities. A comparison between the conductor strategy and the dominator strategy is outlined as follows.

Two strategies of platform leadership

	Conductor Strategy	Dominator Strategy
Definition	The platform leader continues to enjoy good outcomes by improving the health of the whole ecosystem	Integrate vertically or horizontally to manage and control the major parts of the business ecosystem
Status	Controlling power is weaker	Controlling power over most parts is strong
Value creation	Conductor creates value with partners	Creates most value on its own
Value returns	Most of the value created stays and is shared in the business ecosystem	Takes most of the profits alone
Focus and task	Create platform and share solutions through network; balance between value creation and sharing	Focus on control and possession; define, possess, and rule the network
Example	eBay	Enron

Conductor Strategy

Using the conductor strategy, the platformer provides the platform and improves the general health of the business ecosystem. In the case of the iPhone or Android platform, the platformers sustain the platform long enough to produce profits by sharing the technology road map with application developers. The characteristics of the conductor strategy are as follows.

1. The platformer mediates the complex relations among platform participants and simplifies their connections. In addition, by providing the platform, the platformer facilitates development of new products more easily. These activities increase the productivity of the business ecosystem.
2. The conductor strategy actualizes technological innovation. It also strengthens ecosystems by allowing the platformer to be a trustworthy guide for participants who are reluctant to respond to new

circumstances. A strong ecosystem has the capability to withstand changes in the external environment. The strength of a platform ecosystem depends on having a stable and predictable platform. Information as to which direction the platform will evolve is shared between the platformer and the developers, making them feel at ease and enabling them to concentrate on innovation. Also, the platform absorbs shocks from external changes, taking some pressure off the developers.

3. The conductor strategy stimulates and vitalizes niche creation by distributing innovative technology to many companies on the platform. Here, niche creation refers to the phenomenon by which new business fields are born in the business ecosystem, based on innovation enabled by the platform.

4. The platformer shares most of the value created with the whole ecosystem. Some portions of the value created is retained for its own prosperity, but the survival and development of other participants in the ecosystem must also be considered. In short, the platformer must find the balance between its need to collect revenue for its own survival, and the survival and development of all partner companies.

Dominator Strategy

The dominator strategy is the strategy used in the piping environment. Market leaders that adopt the dominator strategy prefer the traditional approach and the advantages of wielding their influence. They try to maximize profits as much as they can. They also try to dominate the value chain, using their important status to control their partners. Especially in the field of online sales, since the market is completely open, if one company can be the gateway, it can control other companies. However, use of the dominator strategy can devastate the ecosystem. The characteristics of the dominator strategy are as follows.

1. The dominator, focusing on vertical or horizontal integration, tries to possess and control most of the value chain which is the

foundation of the ecosystem. Traditionally, the leading company expands its business into fields that add value. Once an economies of scale is accomplished, the leading company then expands its business vertically and horizontally.

2. In the traditional industrial trajectory, one large company dominates most of the value chain. Once the dominator monopolizes in this way, the development of the business ecosystem becomes difficult, because its lifeline must include variety and innovation.

In today's modern business world, the role of the platformer will continue to become more important. However, there still are some occasions in which the dominator strategy is desirable. When innovation is slow, when investment should be concentrated, when mediation is required for smooth business transactions among partners, when the cost of trade between companies is too high, and when the risk of innovation cannot be reduced by expansion and diffusion — all these are occasions that call for the dominator strategy.

When innovation happens slowly, frequent development of new products is difficult. Therefore, it is not necessary to stimulate innovation from the partners in the ecosystem. Also, small businesses may lack the capacity to take the risk of large-scale projects. If mediation is required or the transaction costs are too high, innovation may actually be more efficient when the dominator executes the plan itself and profits from it. In some cases, it is difficult to produce the desired outcome even if the risk is shared by many small businesses that want to enjoy the advantages of expansion and diffusion. For example, the development of new medicine in the pharmaceutical industry requires concentrated investment rather than expansion and diffusion.

Value Creation and Sharing

An effective conductor strategy emphasizes two points. These are value creation in the business ecosystem and sharing of the value created.

Maximization of Value Creation

Platformers must maximize value creation by offering a useful platform to business ecosystem participants. At the same time, win–win situations must be set up by proper distribution of the value created to all participants. If the leading company cannot provide a way to create value efficiently, it will have a hard time attracting participants and keeping them in the ecosystem. In the same way, if the leading company does not provide a way of sharing the created value, it may have temporary success, but eventually its partners will exit the ecosystem.

The conductor must lead the value creation of the ecosystem by offering a platform. Ecosystem members can approach the platform through an interface, which is the method of connecting with the platform. Standard technology in the IT field, such as Internet, is also a sort of interface. If a partner connects to the platform through the interface, something valuable can be added to the market by combining its own products or ideas with what are being offered on the platform.

Companies utilizing the platform develop their products, taking the interface as the starting point of value creation activity. The platform is the means by which the conductor shares the ecosystem and the created value. Microsoft's Windows operating system is a typical platform. Windows provides program developers with an interface to hardware. Therefore, program developers can concentrate on their own application without worrying about the details of hardware.

All platforms offer one or more of the three properties for all business partners to expand and share: physical properties such as high-efficiency production lines, intellectual property like a software platform, and financial property like a venture capitalist's investment portfolio.

Physical properties include large-scale manufacturing or retail property (retail chains like Walmart), direct customer links (Dell Computers), and the role of the hub in network integration. The hub strategy of Dell stems from its ability to utilize direct connections with the customer network. These connections create customer hubs of enormous value to the company and its suppliers.

Intellectual properties include standards (Linux), productivity tools (Visual Studio), shared Internet components (Java Beans), and information hubs (Google, eBay). Resulting from standards, platform participants can use a database or directory right away. If there is no standard for the information to be stored, the platformer should produce one. Financial properties mean investment in new companies, takeover of complementary companies, and other related matters.

The platformer provides the interface for outside individuals or companies to use these properties for the purpose of value creation. This interface induces the complementors' participation, and their participation becomes the base of value creation.

Survival through Sharing and Distribution

If there is no proper sharing and distribution, platform partners will face difficulties; to resolve the situation, they may even move to another competing platform. If there is no competing platform, or every platform is low on sharing and distribution, as we have seen in the examples of AOL and Enron, the whole ecosystem will collapse.

A wise platformer must adopt the conductor strategy, in which the profit collected is only as much as it needs, and the rest or most of the value created by the business ecosystem, is left to other members of the ecosystem. Value distributed this way ensures the members' survival and promotes innovation activity.

In a healthy platform, the balance issue must be resolved of how much the conductor's share should be to ensure its survival, and how much should remain in the ecosystem. The best solution is to increase the number of participants. As the number of users increases, the value of the platform increases exponentially. Since the cost does not increase much, the surplus value increases, and the platform leader can share this surplus value with platform partners. Many companies failed when the Internet was booming because although the rising number of users increased the value of the platform, the platform management costs increased more than expected.

eBay is a company that successfully creates value and shares it with its ecosystem partners. eBay provides these partners with various value creation strategies. For example, the Trading Assistants service helps new seller's listings. eBay's Turbo-Lister service traces and manages thousands of listings on the site. Since these services increase the productivity of the participants, they are very attractive tools for potential users. eBay has implemented a performance evaluation standard to increase the stability of the system. By letting buyers and sellers evaluate each other and by making the ranking public, the platform secures the user's trust. Sellers with constant good reviews attain the status of power sellers, and those with bad reviews naturally die out.

Incentives such as power seller status strengthen seller standards, eventually benefiting the whole ecosystem. This evaluation system gives users a responsibility to maintain order. This voluntary maintenance of order by users saves eBay the costs of monitoring and soliciting feedback.

eBay shows an excellent sense of balance in the matter of sharing created value with ecosystem members. It charges low fees to users when they control trade activities. eBay charges low commission, no more than 10% of sales. This is very low compared with the 30–70% margin most retail businesses charge. By sharing value this way, eBay is expanding its healthy ecosystem and ensuring its sustainability.

Understand the Nature of the Business

The Nature of the Business and Killer Contents

'What is this platform to society and the customer?'
'Why do we do this? Why do we exist?'
'What inconvenience would customers experience if this company disappeared?'

These are the questions to ask in order to determine the nature of the business, which is key to selecting the killer contents. The company's contribution to society and mission is related to the nature of the business. The mission of a platform company relates to its purpose for existence in society. When a platform is established, its meaning in society should be considered in order for the company to have direction and a chart for moving forward. Determining the nature of the business is quite simple. It can be easily answered by the questions above. The nature of the business is also related to its killer contents.

Competition between platforms is largely a fight over who has more attractive solutions to offer. The killer contents should be developed through an understanding of the nature of the business. If the set of solutions the platform has to offer is attractive, the competitive edge of the platform improves. Therefore, if the platform manager does not understand the nature of the business, no appropriate platform management strategy can be implemented. The platform manager must constantly monitor if the mission is being accomplished. The mission of the platform company must include a value proposition and a series of benefits that customers may enjoy or desperately need.

According to Peter Drucker, the mission statement should be available in written form, and it should be based on the following 5 questions:

— What is the business?
— Who are the customers?
— What is the value provided to the customers?
— What is our outcome?
— What is our plan?

These 5 questions are important for a company's business, customers, values, future, and ability to respond to change.

The Nature of the Business and Ecosystem Strategy

On the platform, ecosystem participants are the principal agents for various solutions to problems. They sometimes offer each other solutions or consume the solutions. Therefore, the platformer must make efforts to improve the killer contents, supporting the ecosystem and the platform. The following two examples provide good models.

Chinese Take-out Service and the Delivery Ecosystem

What is the nature of Chinese delivery food? It is 'peace'. People get upset when they are hungry. When people are upset, fights break out. Therefore, Chinese delivery food, which is affordable and delivered quickly, satisfies the empty stomach; it can be viewed as a peace evangelist.

From this point of view, the killer content of Chinese delivery food is speed, especially the speed of delivery. The Chinese delivery food platform is the place that connects the delivery ecosystem and the customer ecosystem. Competition among Chinese delivery food platforms is a fight for the fastest delivery time and the solution of good service. If a delivery is late, the customers get hungry and try other solutions. Therefore, the reason for the deliveryman's existence is speed. The Chinese delivery food platform provides the solution to the problem of hunger: deliver the food to the customer as fast as possible in order to give them peace.

Many Chinese delivery restaurants strive to improve the delivery ecosystem. A successful Chinese delivery restaurant has many deliverymen who know the nature of the business and its relation to the killer contents (speed). Customers may be impressed by these deliverymen to the point that they let others know about the restaurant, and as a result, the number of orders increases. There are good reasons and factors governing this success.

EDLP Solution of Walmart and Merchandising Ecosystem

Walmart's platform is the space connecting the merchandising ecosystem (supply) and the customer ecosystem (demand). It provides solutions to the problem of goods for its customers. Walmart's mission of EDLP (everyday low price) provides customers with many goods at low prices. Its goods are available for cheaper prices, because they are sourced from all over the world. As a result of this mission, customers must endure the long drive to the store. Therefore, Walmart puts the emphasis on improvement of the merchandising ecosystem, which provides products of good quality at low prices.

Platform Architecture Design

The platform should be designed to encourage interplay between participants. The key to the ecosystem is good partnerships. Another key element is that it connects and integrates the functions of different organizations. For this purpose, the platformer company should plan an architecture that will retain interested parties in the value chain, overcoming the tendency to pursue short-term interests.

Business ecosystems are composed of elements that can be remembered through the acronym SPICE (Sisodia *et al.*, 2007). SPICE stands for the essential components of the business ecosystem, such as cooperating Society, Partners, Investors, Customers, and Employees.

Another acronym, CPNT/D (Contents, Platform, Network, Terminal or Device) in the analysis of the mobile platform structure suggests the necessity of integrated management of the contents, network, and devices.

Users of mobile devices need support for software, such as apps and music contents. This explains why the initial MP3 music platform failed in Korea, where the first MP3 player was invented. Unlike iPod and iTunes, the MP3 music industry in Korea only had a device and did not have enough contents prepared to establish the platform.

An architecture that includes all interested parties evolves into its ideal form when the SPICE elements and CPNT/D are integrated, as in the following model of the cross-network (see: Model for platform architecture).

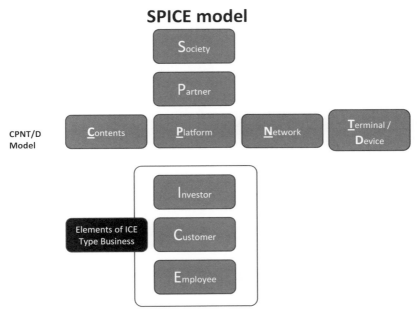

Model for platform architecture

ICE and SPICE Management Models

The ICE management model is a "stand-alone" management model. By contrast, the SPICE model is an ecosystem management model reflecting the interplay among interested parties. Rather than "ICE" cold competition, the SPICE model emphasizes the role of "SPICE"-society, platform, and partner as well as investor, customer, and employee. Since ecosystem management is the creation of business for society rather than individuals, efforts toward peaceful coexistence with other organizations must be made.

From the ecosystem's point of view, both cooperation and competition are needed on the platform. In recent years, business competition has evolved from competition based on products of individual companies to competition between business ecosystems. Therefore, managers must adopt more cooperative strategies than competitive strategies.

In the structure of a business ecosystem, the survival of an organization is highly influenced by ecosystem-related organizations or value chain members. In the stand-alone model, external environmental elements are considered beyond the control of business managers. However, in the ecosystem model, external ecosystems are considered valuable, and it is important to utilize or nurture them through cooperative interplay. Therefore, individuals in the ecosystem evolve together through competition and cooperation. For organizations that are isolated and lacking relationships within the ecosystem, survival may be difficult.

Ecosystem models can be classified as follows: those in which external resources are collected and utilized passively, and those that actively support, nurture, and cultivate the use of external resources. The former is the hunting ecosystem model, and the latter is the cultivation ecosystem model. The hunting model focuses on the passive selection and utilization of existing external resources. The leader in this scenario is usually a dominator. The leader chooses talent from outside the company rather than cultivating internal resources. A leader of the dominator type tends to enjoy the winner-take-all monopoly game, in which the maximum amount of the existing pie is taken as its own resources.

By contrast, the cultivation model is based on the idea that the business ecosystem should be cultivated through seeding, nurturing, and harvesting. The "pie" is enlarged with a long-term perspective, and the leader acts as a conductor who nurtures the ecosystem rather than as a dominator. Through this process, the space in which ecosystem members play becomes the platform.

Comparison of key business management and platform ecosystem management styles

	ICE Model (Hunting Model)	SPICE Model (Cultivation Model)
Business model	Produce-and-sell business model	Mating-and-pollination business model
A range of interested business parties	ICE (cold-blooded management)	SPICE (management contributing to society and partners as well as ecosystem elements)
Business border	Clear border Hunting mode as "stand-alone" model	Business ecosystem management overcoming border Cultivation mode as "flower and bee" model
Trade and interface	The procurement relations between the producing and consuming agents.	The co-evolution and co-development relation of ecosystem members
System openness	Closed system Walled garden	Open system Open garden
Role of large and small companies	Economy and competitive edge of the large group is emphasized	Role of small businesses emphasized. (To build a big building, the sand is needed between the stones.)
Competition & cooperation	Limitless competition of the closed system	Competition and cooperation of the open system
Role of key business manager	Dominator strategy Manager controls the profits	Conductor strategy (general manager) Manager is the architect making the ecosystem attractive
Example	Battle of devices	War of ecosystems: platform wars

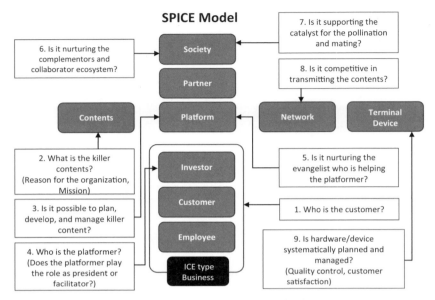

Platform architecture and strategic checkpoints

Manage Platform Boundaries

A horizontal industry structure, unlike vertical integration, lends itself to fierce and indiscrete competition. In this competitive mode, companies strive for survival. After a while, the competitors who achieve superiority in terms of production costs, quality, technology, and service lead the market.

Once a company dominates the market, it seeks the opportunity to expand vertically. Microsoft and Intel followed this pattern once they dominated their supply chain. Intel expanded its territory from the microprocessor to the design and the assembly of motherboard modules. Therefore, the business of system assembly companies like HP, Dell Computers, and IBM were greatly undermined. In addition, Intel added more and more functions to its microprocessors whenever it introduced a new microprocessor. These functions were usually provided by software suppliers, so Intel's actions encroached upon the territory of its competitors.

Microsoft, after dominating the PC operating system market, also expanded its turf to applied software, network services, web browsers, server operating systems, and so on. In short, Microsoft became more like the IBM of the past. Microsoft is a dominator in its industry, monopolizing the profits.

Intel and Microsoft, as platform leaders in the PC market, constantly expanded the boundaries of their platforms. This strategy may increase convenience and efficiency, but it also provoked controversy about oppression, lack of diversity, and control over the competition.

As mentioned earlier, in the conductor strategy, value creation is important, but value distribution and peaceful coexistence with ecosystem members are also important. Value distribution is not only about the commission rate, but also about respecting boundaries. The conductor strategy acknowledges the independence of partner businesses. Indiscrete invasion of a partner's business field is a typical dominator strategy. By contrast, a conductor must consider how to divide the labor with its partners for the value creation of the whole business ecosystem. A platform may expand in a certain direction when the leader thinks the field is mature enough. Microsoft Office is one example.

The following tenets are necessary for good boundary management on a platform: 1. Protect key technology, but share interface technology; 2. Sacrifice short-term interests for the common interests of the industry or ecosystem; 3. Do not invade the partner's turf; 4. Support the protection of the intellectual property of complementors.

Develop Platform Strategy

In decision-making related to platform development, the platform strategy should be based on the question, "How open will it be?" The following factors must be considered when developing a platform strategy.

First, a clear decision about the roles of the platformer and the participating companies is necessary. In the beginning phase of the platform, the role of the platformer is very important. It involves planning of the platform's architecture and governance with consideration of the market and its particular environment. When high standards and quality are important, the platform should be more closed, and when diversity and the number of participants are important, it should be more open. In addition, how the platform creates value in the industry should be analyzed. Obtaining economies of scale by attracting more users may be important, or the connection and interplay among users may be more important. In any case, the decision should be made with the expectation that cooperation among users will be prioritized.

Secondly, a platform, once it is up and running, is a system in which all participants create value together. Therefore, it should not be considered the property of a particular company. The platform increases in value as participating individuals or companies give their best. Therefore, they should be granted autonomy to do their best. At the same time, it does not mean that the platformer should do nothing. The platformer must constantly modify the platform architecture and governance depending on the market response and varying circumstances in the growth process.

Today's App Store would not have started without Apple or Amazon. However, if these companies did not respect the autonomy of participating companies in the platform, the success of the App store would have been limited. The dominator strategy of the past, "the main company orders and the participating companies execute", should be changed to a conductor strategy of "the main company and participating companies plan and execute cooperatively".

Chapter 07

Platform Evolution
and the Future of Platforms

- How Will Platforms Evolve?
- Disappearing Barriers
- Building Online Platforms
- The War among Online Platforms

Certain things precede strategy planning and predicting about a platform. It is important to understand that company-to-company, person-to-person interplay and collaboration only became possible with the development of information technology. It is also necessary to understand how workplace environments have changed, since the platform as a business format arose naturally from changes in the business environment. Here, we examine changes in the management environment and the circumstances that brought about the platform business phenomenon.

How Will Platforms Evolve?

Changes in management environment that have influenced the advent of platform business and will continue to influence its future are outlined in this section.

The Rise of Information Technology

As mentioned earlier, with the development of information technology, fast and efficient collaboration on a large scale including hundreds, thousands, or even millions of participants became possible. This trend is expected to continue and platform business is to become more developed. Even those businesses that are considered unsuitable for the platform mode may become suitable with the help of information technology.

For example, in the past, work related to accounting and finance was thought to be best executed within the company. However, outsourcing to professionals in the areas of accounting, finance, and even human resources is becoming very popular. Businesses that engage in outsourcing may, in a certain way, be considered a platform. Just as Apple's App Store provides a completely new business in the platform mode, these outsourcing businesses offer services through platform, which previously accomplished within companies. Many businesses may be transformed into platform mode through information technology. This transformation will be a great help in discovering future business opportunities.

Decreasing Knowledge Asymmetry

A decrease in "knowledge asymmetry" brought the environment in which individuals and companies can gather to create more value together. 'Knowledge asymmetry' refers to the inequality of knowledge possessed by the parties involved in a certain industry or field. Unlike in the past, many individuals and small companies nowadays have better capabilities than a large company in certain respects. This is the decreasing knowledge asymmetry or equalization of knowledge phenomenon.

Platform businesses thrive when participating individuals and companies have something to contribute. For example, Apple created the App Store platform rather than developing apps for itself because apps developed by outside developers create greater value. The large number of outside developers enables the firm to provide a wide variety of apps. Variety and quantity are not the only advantages of the App Store. In many cases, apps developed by outside developers are of better quality than those developed by Apple.

Knowledge equalization is evident in the software industry: the idea or knowledge is more important than large-scale investment. The App Store provides an infrastructure to developers with excellent abilities. By attracting such talent through its infrastructure, Apple is creating value. InnoCentive is another example of this kind of business. This decreasing knowledge asymmetry is expected to continue, and new platforms will emerge in areas where ideas and knowledge are important.

Sharing and Co-utilization of Property

Sharing and co-utilization of resources is becoming more important than possession of resources. Platform businesses create value by sharing their platforms. For example, imagine a scenario in which Amazon uses its electronic commerce platform only for its own sales, not sharing it with outside sellers. Imagine if Apple tried to develop all apps for the iPhone by itself. From these examples, the importance of sharing and co-utilization becomes apparent.

Of course, sharing is not always ideal. Amazon shares its platform but maintains control over the platform. Apple is similar in this. Moreover, opening the platform to outsiders can be harmful as in the case of motor platforms. Nevertheless, companies can create great value through sharing and utilizing their properties.

Disappearing Barriers

Platform Openness

We now examine the role of platform openness. Facebook is a typical example of a platform where openness plays a key role. The Facebook platform, especially Facebook Connect, is extremely open. Through Facebook Connect, the boundaries between Facebook and other sites are destroyed. If Facebook is considered a network, we see that its network has the capacity for limitless expansion through Facebook Connect. This network externality has enormous value.

Large-Scale Collaboration Using Information Technologies

Why is platform openness applauded? The most important reason is that connecting with various businesses and individuals becomes easy with the use of information technology. In the past, the costs of coordination and conducting business transactions necessary to connect various businesses were prohibitive. Transaction costs, in addition to those associated with the financial transaction for exchange of goods and services include the cost of finding trade partners, the cost of communication with them, and the cost of monitoring them. These transaction costs can be very high, especially when related to complex activities like R&D.

The situation has changed with the use of new information technology like the Internet . It is now possible to connect millions of people and institutes efficiently to cooperate on various projects. Changes in collaboration due to information technology can be summed up in the abbreviation "3S", as explained in the following three points of change.

Changes in collaboration through the development of information technology:

The Three S's

There are three points of change related to business collaboration brought about by information technology:

— **The Scale of Collaboration**: Global cooperation is now possible.

— **The Sophistication of Collaboration**: It is not simply an exchange of documents; commerce and complex R&D are now possible through sophisticated electronic platforms.

— **The Speed of Collaboration**: Before companies begin the collaboration process, they must have a common understanding of the business and its partners. In traditional environments, this took a long time, but today it can be rapidly accomplished at a distance through systematic computer connections.

As more participants use the platform, their unit costs of doing business decrease, and a larger variety of services becomes available. Therefore, the value of the platform for users increases. An open platform, compared with a closed platform, obtains higher value since more connections between businesses and individuals are possible.

Initially, open platform management was very costly. For example, in the past, electronic commerce was conducted without the Internet. Business was conducted through telephone and fax, and the costs were high. These days, due to the development of information technology, large-scale collaboration can be accomplished at a low cost. As a result, the value of the open platform can be increased following that low cost. This explains the popularity of electronic commerce and social network services that are influenced by the Internet.

Open vs. Closed Platforms

On the continuum, Apple is closer to a closed platform, and Facebook is closer to an open platform. The question then arises: between open and closed platforms, is one always better than the other? The answer is that it depends on the kind of platform and its goal. If the goal of the platform is to attract participants for the purpose of information exchange, as in the case of Facebook, then a completely open platform is a good policy. However, when the standard and quality of participants is most important, as in the case of the Apple App Store, a partially closed policy is desirable.

In addition, if the value of the platform stems from physical and standardized commodities, a closed platform is appropriate. However, if the value of the platform lies in the connection among the participants or the diversity of the service, an open platform is more appropriate. For example, in designing a car, the car platform and major parts, such as engines, must satisfy a complex and strict standard. Therefore, a closed policy limiting the company's cooperation with only selected partners will increase the value of the platform. On the other hand, connecting more people is the value of Facebook. Therefore, in these cases, an open policy is advisable.

Platform openness is an advantage in terms of platform competition, especially in cases where the platforms are similar. Cases of competition based on openness include: Google Play competing with Apple's App Store, eBay competing with Amazon, and Myspace competing with Facebook. In these cases, the company that gains supremacy first in terms of numbers of participants earns the advantageous position due to network externalities. An open platform is more advantageous than a closed one because it is easier to attract participants. On the other hand, in the case of platforms the importance of which lies in cooperation and following a complex standard, the procurement of participants is less important.

Platform as an Open Ecosystem

For a successful platform, network externality is key. The business ecosystem should be structured as an open one in which new value is welcomed from the outside and accepted. Openness here means that there are no barriers to participation. Therefore, any interested parties can participate and become part of the ecosystem of the platform. To extend the nature analogy, even if the garden is beautiful, if it is confined inside the greenhouse surrounded by walls, no bees and butterflies can come and make fruit. In the same sense, the platform thrives when new services and products are constantly introduced by new participants. The open garden model works best.

Building Online Platforms

In the initial days of platforms being established online, many of them died out through competition. They can be classified into four groups based on their date of establishment. First, there were platforms based on search engines like Google, Baidu, and Naver. Next came platforms based on electronic commerce like Amazon, Alibaba, and G-market. The third platform group is based on social network services (SNS). Facebook, WeChat, and WhatsApp are examples. Finally, there are smartphone-based platforms such as the iPhone and the Android phone. These four kinds of platforms are discussed in more detail in the following section.

Search Engine-Based Platforms

The value of platforms based on search engines is information provision. Among the various search engines, Yahoo took the lead in the beginning, but Google has supremacy these days. In Korea, Naver has been unrivaled for a long time, but it has reached its limit since platform competition is expanding to the global market.

In addition, search engines have expanded their search range from webpages to maps and images. A most interesting development is the ability of these search engines to provide related offline service based on map services. With an accurate and precise map, navigation services are possible. In addition, using a map and location information, they can provide location-based services (LBS) such as restaurant searches. The Uber service, which has become popular recently, is only possible because of the accuracy of map services like Google Maps.

Electronic Commerce-Based Platforms

For platforms based on electronic commerce, the value comes from the ability to purchase the products that users want in good condition and to provide fast delivery. In the beginning stages of electronic commerce, various business models such as eBay and Amazon competed in the market. More recently, competition has become more complicated with the increasing popularity of social commerce based on group buying. In this context, the most powerful platform worldwide is Amazon, which sells goods directly. In addition, Amazon's platform provides a wide range of services, including contents through their own electronic hardware: the Kindle.

Social Network Service-Based Platforms

The major advantage of a social network service-based platform like Facebook, Instagram, and WhatsApp is the information it provides about users. People share various and detailed information. They leave information at such a level of detail about when they did something, what they ate, what they worry about, and whom they talked to that it is almost unthinkable. The basic value of SNS lies in the exchange of this information with other people. Based on this information, social network platforms can provide value that other platforms cannot.

Smart Phone-Based Platforms

The value of a smartphone-based platform such as the iPhone or Android is communication and content provision. Smartphones are used for the consumption of contents like news or videos, social network services, internet searches for goods in which they are interested, and location-based services like map services. Therefore, smartphone-based platforms often act as interfaces between customers and services provided by other platforms.

The War among Online Platforms

The Inevitable Clash

The four kinds of online platforms mentioned above could have coexisted since their origins were very different, and their territories were clearly separated. However, the possibility of war has arisen recently since the advent of integration among these platforms. It seems that conflict among these platforms is inevitable as they expand their territories. In a symbolic gesture that reflects this inevitability, Google deleted Amazon apps from its Play Store[1] to discourage users from purchasing contents other than those provided by Google. As Amazon silently launched its own app store, Amazon is in direct competition with Google Play store, Google, which has a history of emphasizing openness and coexistence, decided to delete all Amazon apps.

Complications

What form of war will take place among these four kinds of platforms?

Google Enters the SNS and Electronic Commerce Industries

Google currently has a search engine, Youtube, and the Android smart phone. Google is trying to expand its service into the areas of social networks and electronic commerce. These efforts have not been successful so far, but Google seems determined to continue. Google has in fact succeeded in increasing the distribution of contents through YouTube. YouTube is the world's largest video distribution platform. It is mainly used for free video consumption at this point, but it can also easily be used for distribution of paid contents or for online commerce.

---

[1] https://techcrunch.com/2014/12/11/google-removes-amazons-app-listing-from-google-play-search-following-addition-of-appstore-instant-video-integrations/

Naver Expands its Territory through Social Network Services

In Korea, Naver established a social network platform by developing Line. Line ranks third after WhatsApp and WeChat worldwide.[2] Naver now maintains two kinds of platforms — a search engine and a SNS, thus holding a more advantageous position in the platform competition. The recent merger of Daum and KakaoTalk is widely considered to be a response to this. When a search engine and SNS are integrated, various synergy effects are possible. For example, the KakaoTaxi service, which is a new service from KakaoTalk, requires accurate map information. Daum provides this information, so KakaoTalk can easily provide the service.

Amazon Obtains a Search Engine

Amazon specializes in electronic commerce but is trying to enter the field of content distribution. As explained earlier, Amazon holds an unrivaled position in the electronic book distribution industry with its Kindle device. Software and application distribution is the next step. Amazon can easily enter this field because electronic book distribution is not so different technologically from the distribution of software and applications in the sense that they are all types of digital information.

Another case of successful expansion is Amazon's product information search engine. Amazon is the platform with the most information about products in the entire world. In addition to price information and product images, Amazon also provides customer reviews of its products. Moreover, the Amazon search engine is optimized for product searches. Thus, many people choose Amazon when they search for products, although they choose Google for general searches. If Amazon continues to expand its search range, a conflict with Google seems inevitable.

---

[2] The number of active monthly users as of January, 2016 is 900 million for WhatsApp, 650 million for WeChat, 212 million for Line, and 48 million for KakaoTalk.

Social Network Services and Social Commerce

The greatest advantage of SNS is its provision of personal and social information about users. Currently, SNS is frequently used for advertisement; SNS providers are now moving into the area of social commerce in addition to advertisement. Here, social commerce does not refer to group buying mentioned earlier. We use the original meaning of social commerce: the utilization of users' social information to enhance their shopping experience.

Information about users' social networks indicates the social groups to which they belong, and the shopping patterns of these groups indicate their tastes. All this data can be utilized for the purposes of commerce. For example, imagine person A has 10 friends with whom he frequently interacts through SNS. If we examine the list of recent purchases of the 10 friends, we can predict what products A might purchase because people in the same social group tend to share the same tastes and shopping patterns. This information can have a tremendous ripple effect. Therefore, when SNS engages in social commerce, conflicts with electronic commerce platforms like Amazon are unavoidable.

SNS may also expand its territory to the area of content distribution. People tend to consume the same contents[3] as their acquaintances. Therefore, social information can be used for increasing content consumption. This battle between SNS, Amazon, and Google for content-related territory is ramping up.

Smartphone-Based Platforms for All Areas

Smartphone-based platforms overlap with other platforms in many areas. In fact, the smartphone itself is the interface with other platforms. For example, to search for information on the smartphone, a user may choose to use Google or Naver search engines; to buy products, the Amazon app, and to access SNS, WhatsApp.

---

[3] Mainly movies, music, or videos. In a broad sense, this software is also included.

Smartphone-based platforms have a competitive edge in terms of creating value because the smartphone itself is the device, and the operating system (iOS or Android) is the interface or gatekeeper. Actually, Apple's App Store or Google's Play Store is the gatekeeper. If the smartphone user purchases contents from the App Store or the Play Store, some of the profit goes to Apple or to Google.

Most value on an online platform comes from the network rather than the solution. Therefore, integration of various platforms is the ideal strategy to create more value. To be more precise, if we can search for information, go shopping, and interact with friends, all on the same device, it would be ideal. Obviously, expansion of territory among online platforms will inevitably result in conflict. We therefore assert that a war among the online platforms is imminent. Attention must be paid to which platform will win the competition, and what strategy each platform should take.

Epilogue

Ecosystemic Capitalism

The decoupling[1] of society and business is ongoing. Previous management strategies involving hunting for resources and institutional management are becoming extinct. Hunting mode management requires social resources to create value; it has the limitation of exhausting and exploiting existing resources.

Therefore, business associates and capitalists must learn the wisdom behind the nurturing of the business ecosystem. Rather than short-term, exploitive management, cultivation of human resources is necessary. Comprehensive, ecosystemic management that meets the needs of society and nurtures resources is vital to our future. The ecosystemic approach to business may be the solution for capitalism-related conflicts such as "Occupy Wall Street". Only ecosystemic capitalism can vitalize business ecosystems and solve problems related to economic polarization.

In ecosystemic capitalism, individual companies must pursue enlightened self-interest indirectly rather than directly. A competitive edge should be sought not only in terms of internal capacity, but also in terms of cooperative relations with the external business ecosystem.

---

[1] Decoupling, in the transportation sense, means the separation and redirection of the cars on a train. In economics, the term refers to a divergence from the general economic trend.

Short-term-oriented business management threatens corporate longevity. Human beings cannot avoid the inevitable: death. A company is a different story. A company can transform itself and be reborn with proper management of the ecosystem.

To refer back to the garden analogy, if many bees surround the flower, the flower will produce fruit and in turn, the health of the ecosystem will improve. Sustainable growth is accomplished through pollination and mating. In the ecosystem, short-term survival is important. However, for long-term vitalization of the field, there should be a harvest in the fall, and seeding should be achieved the following year. To sustain the ecosystem, a constantly repeating cycle of regeneration and harvest should occur.

In the business ecosystem as well, seeding must occur in spring (creativity), trees must grow during summer (market opportunity), harvest must take place in the fall (productivity), and preparations must be made for next year (feedback).

Companies that have experienced smooth and steady growth may suddenly collapse following a failure to adjust to the changing environment and ecosystem. As in Darwin's natural selection theory, if a company fails to change with the environment, the ecosystem no longer selects it. Therefore, constant observation of changes in the environment and vigilant corresponding adjustments are necessary.

The greatest conflict in any ecosystem is between productivity and creativity. Productivity is related to the capability with the existing market, and creativity is related to the ability to blaze a trail in the future market. The ecosystem improves when there is a balance between productivity and creativity.

Harmonious evolution of these two abilities is achieved through constant observation. Productivity can increase through improved organizational capability. Creativity evolves through the dynamic capability of the firm and its ability to respond to environmental changes.

Platform business is expected to play a key role in the transformation of the world's economy to ecosystemic capitalism, because the key to platform business is cooperation among various businesses to create value on the platform. The transformation to a platform-based economy is also a big change in the business environment. Businesses should recognize these environmental changes, and decide how to adjust accordingly.

Bibliography

Books

Chesbrough, H. W. (2003), *The Open Innovation: The New Imperative for Creating and Profiting from Technology*, Harvard Business School Press, Boston, MA.

Gawer, A. and M. A. Cusumano (2002), *Platform Leadership: How Intel, Microsoft, and Cisco Drive Industry Innovation*, Harvard Business School Press, Boston, MA.

Iansiti, M. and R. Levien (2004), *The Keystone Advantage: What the New Dynamics of Business Ecosystems Mean for Strategy, Innovation, and Sustainability*, Harvard Business School Press, Boston, MA.

Kim, Kyung Joon (2006), *The Great Company, Learn from Rome*, Won & Books.

Kim, Myung Ho (2012), *The Story of Chinese People*, Hangilsa.

Kwak, Seung Joon *et al.* (2012), *Smart Capitalism 5.0: Excite the Industry Ecosystem*, Nanam.

Meyer, M. H. and A. P. Lehnerd (1997), *The Power of Product Platforms: Building Value and Cost Leadership*, Free Press, New York, NY.

Moore, J. F. (1996), *The Death of Competition: Leadership and Strategy in the Age of Business Ecosystems*, Harper Business, New York, NY.

Samsung Economics Research Institute (2008), *The Rise of the Global Network Industry Model*, Samsung Economic Research Institute (SERI).

Sangsaeng Management Research (2006), *Sangsaeng Management*, Kimyoungsa.

Sisodia, R., Sheth, J., and Wolfe, D. B. (2007), *Firms of Endearment: The Pursuit of Purpose and Profit*, Wharton School Publishing, Upper Saddle River, NJ.

Academic Journals

Caillaud, B. and Jullien, B. (2003), "Chicken & egg: Competition among intermediation service providers," *RAND Journal of Economics*, pp. 309–328.

Dhanaraj, C. and Parkhe, A. (2006), "Orchestrating innovation networks," *Academy of Management Review*, 31 (3), pp. 659–669.

Eisenhardt, K. M. and Galunic, D. C. (2000), "Co-evolving: At last, a way to make synergies work," *Harvard Business Review*, 78 (1), pp. 91–101.

Eisenmann, T., Parker, G., and Van Alstyne, M. (2006), "Strategies for two-sided markets," *Harvard Business Review*, 84 (10), p. 92.

Evans, D. S. (2003), "The antitrust economics of multi-sided platform markets," *Yale Journal on Regulation*, 20, pp. 325–382.

Hagiu, A. (2007), "Merchant or two-sided platform?," *Review of Network Economics*, 6 (2), pp. 115–133.

Huston, L. and Sakkab, N. (2006), "Connect and develop," *Harvard Business Review*, 84 (1), pp. 58–66.

Kim, Ki-Chan (2009), "Research development strategy and the platform leadership from the business ecosystem perspective: Large & small companies' cooperation and their research and development," *Small Business Research*, 32 (2), pp. 157–176.

Lechner, C. and Dowling, M. (2003), "Firm networks: External relationships as sources for the growth and competitiveness of entrepreneurial firms," *Entrepreneurship & Regional Development*, 15 (1), pp. 1–26.

Levine, S. and White, P. E. (1961), "Exchange as a conceptual framework for the study of inter-organizational relationships," *Administrative Science Quarterly*, 5 (4), pp. 583–601.

Nalebuff, B. J., and Brandenburger, A. M. (1997), "Co-opetition: Competitive and cooperative business strategies for the digital economy," *Strategy & Leadership*, 25 (6), pp. 28–33.

Rigby, D. and Zook, C. (2002), "Open-market innovation," *Harvard Business Review*, 80 (10), pp. 80–89.

Rochet, J. C. and Tirole, J. (2003), "Platform competition in two-sided markets," *Journal of the European Economic Association*, 1 (4), pp. 990–1209.

Newspapers and Magazines

Herald Economy 2014/8/4, "Xiaomi shock, win the Samsung in China," http://biz.heraldcorp.com/view.php?ud+20140805000041

Im, Il (2012), "Open the platform, the win-win game starts," Dong-A Business Review (DBR), No.111, pp.40–46.

Joongang Daily, 2014/11/7, "Market share of Xiaomi in China and the Samsung," http://article.joins.com/news/article/article.asp?tpta;_id=16339932

Kim, Ki-Chan (2014), "Let's embrace bees and flowers like the orchard: Let's get out of the lost humanity," Dong-A Business Review (DBR), No. 148, pp. 44–56.

Tabarrok, Alex, "Jean Tirole and Platform Markets," Marginal Revolution, on October 13, 2014, https://marginalrevolution.com/marginalrevolution/2014/10/tirole-and-platform-markets.html

Techcrunch, 2014/12/11, "Google removes Amazon's app listing from Google Play," https://techcrunch.com/2014/12/11/google-removes-amazons-app-listing-from-google-play-search-following-addition-of-appstore-instant-video-integrations/

TechHolic, 2014/8/18, "From imitation to the face of the Samsung, the growth story of Xiaomi," http://techholic.co.kr/archives/20556

Reports, Websites, and Others

Elop, Stephen, Nokia CEO, 2011/06/01, "It's not a battle of devices, It's a war of ecosystems," (video).

IBM Annual report, 2011, https://www.ibm.com/investor/pdf/2011_ibm_annual.pdf

Kemp, Simon, 2014/08/26, "Chat apps continue growth," https://wearesocial.com/us/blog/2014/08/chat-apps-continue-growth